CO**MING**
FULL CİRCLE

Books by Lynn Andrews

Medicine Woman

Spirit Woman (previously published
as *Flight Of The Seventh Moon*)

Jaguar Woman

Star Woman

Crystal Woman

Windhorse Woman

The Woman Of Wyrrd

Teachings Around The Sacred Wheel

The Power Deck, Cards Of Wisdom

The Mask Of Power

Shakkai

Woman At The Edge Of Two Worlds

Woman At The Edge Of Two Worlds Workbook

Walk In Balance

Dark Sister

Walk In Spirit

Love And Power

Love And Power Workbook

Tree Of Dreams

Writing Spirit

COMING FULL CIRCLE

Ancient Teachings
for a
Modern World

LYNN ANDREWS

RAINBOW RIDGE
BOOKS

Cover and interior design by Frame25 Productions
Cover photo © Triff c/o Shutterstock.com

Published by:
Rainbow Ridge Books, LLC
140 Rainbow Ridge Road
Faber, Virginia 22938
434-361-1723

If you are unable to order this book from your local
bookseller, you may order directly from the distributor.

Square One Publishers, Inc.
115 Herricks Road
Garden City Park, NY 11040
Phone: (516) 535-2010
Fax: (516) 535-2014
Toll-free: 877-900-BOOK

Visit the author at:
www.lynnandrews.com

Library of Congress Cataloging-in-Publication Data applied for.

ISBN 978-1-937907-01-3

10 9 8 7 6 5 4 3

Printed on acid-free recycled paper in the United States of America

To my readers: please understand that the names and places in this book have been changed to protect the privacy and safety of those involved.

Through the Centuries

you make power with your song
with your song

when you make power with your song
bristlecone pine

power your song
old world or modern times

❧

I am thinking of the wilderness again.
You are far away, beyond the desert.
When I walk in the hills, the old songs
enter in. Stone, dirt, shadow.
Blackberry branches across the path.
Here is the sun on my face. Here is the wind near your body.
Morning bird whistles if I listen close in town.
I make this poem with the joy that has resounded
through the centuries. Just now, a siren in the distance.
And now, another hidden bird begins.

—Jack Crimmins

Dedication and Acknowledgements

To the Sisterhood of the Shields for sharing the mystery and your extraordinary wisdom and for having faith in me.

To Clariss Ritter for a superb job of editing and pulling together my never-ending ideas and the disparate tapestry of language within which I live.

Because of my teachers, my daughter, Vanessa, my patient and loving friends, Mike, and my family of staff and students, this book became a joy to write. A special thank you to my agent, Devra Ann Jacobs, and my publisher, Bob Friedman.

Contents

Prologue

Early in my work with my teachers in the Sisterhood of the Shields, I dreamed that I would find a way to honor the gifts that these women of such varied cultures had bestowed on me. How could I explain my ability to see lights around people? How could I share the mysteries that I had experienced? The more I looked for answers, the more I looked at the human condition and the meaning of life. I began to explore the lives and teachings of religious people, wise ones, writers, artists of many different beliefs. I knew that I was a writer. I hoped that I could bring a new way of "seeing" to others, so I climbed into the vast expanse of the conscious and unconscious world.

Since my first dreams of creating a school and being an author, I have written many books, each centered on a particular theme and different teaching. Each book tells the story of my experiences with my teachers. Each story contains a single thread of learning. With this new book, I am able to tie together the fibers of many stories and journeys to share the lessons I have learned with extraordinary women. These very different cultural experiences have empowered me in my struggle to manifest into words what I have learned and dreamed.

May you have your own dreams and awaken to your new understanding!

Introduction

"The End of Days: Where Do We Go from Here?"

Everyone today wants answers. Wherever I travel, meeting people from all walks of life all over the world, I find most often that people today are exploring their reasons for living.

They ask me, "How can I learn more about God and myself? How can I learn more about profound spirituality? I want to learn about the great masters and the women of power. What did they teach you and how did you learn about higher consciousness?"

These seem to be such simple questions. But the answers are complex.

When I began my apprenticeship to Agnes Whistling Elk and Ruby Plenty Chiefs thirty years ago, I had no idea that they were part of a very private and anonymous gathering of elder women of high degree from various native cultures around the world. Later, after I was initiated into their circle—the Sisterhood of the Shields—as a full member, Agnes and Ruby would send me off to study with one or another of these beautiful women.

With Agnes and Ruby, I traveled to Australia to apprentice with Ginevee, an Aboriginal woman of very high degree. I traveled to the jungles of the Yucatán to apprentice with Zoila, a *curendera* of Mayan descent. I traveled to Nepal to apprentice with Ani, a Nepalese hill woman of immense power and wisdom. I have traveled all over the world to study and work with indigenous women healers from many different cultures, all members of the Sisterhood of the Shields.

It has been my considerable privilege to write of my experiences with a number of these women, but not all. Some of them prefer to have our work together held only amongst the Sisterhood, each for her own very respected reasons. Some prefer to remain completely anonymous. Some live in countries where the practice of their beliefs is prohibited by repressive governments and to write of them could expose them to personal danger.

In this book, however, I have the great honor of introducing you to a number of these women about whom I have not previously written, as well as sharing with you additional stories with several of them. Each new story of the Sisterhood is accompanied by an article that grows out of our experiences in the modern world, yours and mine, and how the teachings these women have gifted to us can be applied to help us move into harmony and a state of grace with the world around us. Both the stories and the articles are designed to make the wisdom of the Sisterhood of the Shields more accessible in our daily lives.

While raised in the culture and traditions of their own indigenous worlds, these women don't follow their native traditions. Rather, theirs are the teachings of the sacred feminine, the firstness of women here on Mother Earth, the ancient goddess teachings as they have been preserved, practiced, guarded and handed down to the Sisterhood from mother to daughter, shaman to apprentice, for many thousands of years, throughout the entire lifespan of the patriarchy. These are the teachings they have given to me, and through me, gifted back to a parched and starving world that hungers for higher spiritual consciousness.

The women of the Sisterhood often tell me that human beings were never intended to live with the amount of chaos and confusion that we face in our world today. Yet here we are, and it is precisely because of the perils we are forced to accept as a 'normal' part of being alive today that sacred teachers have walked out of the deserts and jungles of the world, down from the high mountaintops and even the cities where they have been forced to live in virtual obscurity in order to remain alive. They are coming forward to return to a world that had once turned its back their ancient teachings that have never failed humanity, the 'wisdom of the ages,' in all of the many different ways it has been practiced across the globe.

This thought, "the wisdom of the ages," gives me a sense of well-being that fills me with the certainty that I am loved, that I am part of a greater world that has survived lifetimes of change through the healing power of love. By opening our hearts and filling them with this love and the wisdom that is born from it, we can draw all of the strength and wisdom we will ever need in life, if only we know how.

Carl Jung was once asked if he believed in God. He answered, "I don't believe. *I know.*" The Sisterhood of the Shields are women who *know*, and in their knowing I have found a greater clarity in life than I have ever before known, a certainty grounded in the very bedrock of the earth upon which we walk, born of the ancient knowledge and understanding of how energy moves in the universe and how to choreograph that energy toward a higher purpose in life.

As my books will attest, my apprenticeship to these women has often been difficult, fraught with struggle and, to my way of thinking, peril. Many people ask me, "Lynn, how could you, a woman of our world, an art dealer from Beverly Hills, endure this? Why did they put you through all of that turmoil?"

The simple answer is that struggle is really the only way we ever learn about ourselves. You can't teach people about themselves by standing at a podium and lecturing. Especially, you cannot teach people how to find trust, how to honor their own personal truth in life, through the never-ending cycle of lecture and testing as they search for the answers they think someone else expects them to give.

The only way to learn about your own higher consciousness is through personal experience. There have been many great teachers throughout the millenniums, and many powerful and wonderful spiritual books have been written from every beautiful religious and spiritual pathway on earth. But you cannot learn about yourself by reading someone else's interpretations of life and the voice of Divine Spirit. You only learn through applying what they have to say to the experiences of your own life to see what holds true and sacred for you. What works for one person may fall completely flat with another, so why would you want to turn the most precious and sacred aspects of your consciousness over to someone else's experience of truth?

The Sisterhood of the Shields believed firmly, they *knew* that the only way I was ever going to learn, the only way I was going to bridge the enormous chasm between the ways they had grown up so very close to the natural world and my life in Western civilization, was through the process of experience. They knew that those experiences had to be forceful enough to grab my undivided attention so that I had no alternative but to listen to my own voice of wisdom and spirit which they coaxed out of me, a voice which gets positively drowned out by the clamor of modern living. It is a voice which I had glimpsed in rare moments but had never really understood how to access. This is the voice of inner, personal truth with which we are all born into this world.

There is no way I could have even begun to understand what it was Ginevee was trying to teach me about myself had all my personal props not been taken away from me, had I not had to learn how to live with almost nothing in the Australian Outback.

I would not have heard what Zoila was trying to teach me about my sacred nature and incredible power as a woman had I not had to struggle through the physically perilous trials with which she had grown up in the wildness of the Yucatán. From the moment that I first met her, she knew what I refused even to look at in myself: that I didn't believe in myself; that I had no sense of own abilities and capabilities; that I secretly felt unworthy of the great gifts of Divine love and wisdom, even of physical abundance, because I had been abused by my father as a child. She also knew that if she confronted me with words about these feelings which I tried so hard to hide, I would never have listened. She knew to put me into positions where I had to fall back on my innate strengths and weaknesses in order to survive. Then she would talk to me about why I had experienced such terror over what many face on a daily basis and handle just fine, and what this could teach me about myself as I moved forward in life.

My teachers in the Sisterhood of the Shields teach through experience. They teach through humor. They teach through giving you only one of two options: look at yourself so that you can learn and grow, or give it up and walk away. I could have walked away many times, and I am so profoundly thankful that I didn't.

When I stand back and look at my many years with them, the hardships I have faced, how hard I have had to work to understand them, both because of language differences and more importantly because they saw things about me that I didn't want to see about myself, I see so clearly the profound wisdom of their ways. Ruby Plenty Chiefs, with her gruff, confrontational demeanor, forced me to focus every aspect of my being. In doing so, she taught me more about trust and love than anyone else I have ever known. It is probably true that I was only able to reach that level of acceptance because of the boundless love and nurturing that I received from Agnes Whistling Elk, but never doubt that Agnes could be as terrorizing as anyone when it was the only way to open me up to accepting the wisdom after which I had so thirsted my entire life.

And they taught me how to laugh at myself, how not to take myself so seriously that there was no room for light to come into my consciousness. There is always tremendous humor in their ways.

When I was working with Ani, Agnes, and Ruby in Nepal, we set out to climb across the high Himalayas into Tibet for a fifty-year gathering of the Sisterhood of the Shields in the Valley of Luctang. After what was, for me, a frightening encounter with the Chinese Red Guard who secured the borders into Tibet, we were progressing well along the trail when all of a sudden the ground began to shake and huge boulders cascaded down from the mountain peaks, completely obscuring the trail ahead of us. I thought that our lives might well be over.

Ani had other ideas. "Well, Lynn," she said, "it appears that the mountain has given you a gift. It has given you an avalanche, perhaps to show you how you block yourself in life."

Okay, I thought. *This avalanche is a gift, to me. Why not?...* as I stared over the precipice at a sheer cliff face that dropped hundreds of feet into the raging waters below.

"We will do a ceremony," she concluded.

Oh, right. "We will do a ceremony." Why didn't I think of that? We'll just levitate these boulders right out of here. . . because there was no way I was willing to face those Chinese soldiers a second time. The women had rubbed dirt on my face and wrapped me in a *pashamina* shawl, disguising me as a local shepherd boy, but no disguise is infallible. Had I, an American woman, been caught trying to sneak into Tibet, I would have been arrested and thrown into a Chinese prison.

We'll do a ceremony.

The only thing you can do in the face of such odds is laugh, laugh at the situation, laugh at yourself, laugh at the absurdity of the odds. Laughter shakes you up and separates you from the enormity of the situation so that you can find clarity in what you have to do.

A ceremony we did do, and we got down off that mountain quite safely.

All of the women of the Sisterhood are so beautiful in their own ways. As I write of the differences among them, I am so amazed at how alike they really are, vastly different in appearance but as one in spirit.

Their experiences in life are different, yet as I have found, in the work of the shaman, power is the same all over the world. Whether I am sitting with Ginevee and other Aboriginal women in the Outback of Australia or with Zoila and the Mayan women of the Yucatán, the language of power is the same. We don't share a common spoken language but we understand each other fully. We understand each other in the world and we understand on the level of symbolism.

Symbolism is not contracted and contrived by words or interpretation. Except when you are dealing with an archetype— a symbol the meaning of which has a universal quality—no two people are going to see the same thing in a symbol. Even our experiences of the significance of an archetype are going to differ. Communicating in the relative world of physical reality is interesting. When you get into the world on the other side of the veil, it's not as difficult because you move through pictures of things, unclouded by words, judgment, criticism or emotion.

"2012" is a year that has been spoken about for centuries, prophesied by the ancient Mayans over a thousand years ago, written about in the Bible and so many of the ancient texts of the world as a time of huge change on planet Earth.

The ancient scrolls which are hidden in the Seven Clay Pots, guarded by the Sisterhood of the Shields for many hundreds of years, call this the "Crossing Times." It is the time of crossing from one level of human consciousness into a new age of wisdom, where the possibilities of all things are within our grasp. Ani and Agnes have both told me that right now, we have the possibility of creating a new world of heightened understanding if that is our choice.

To the Sisterhood, "2012," the so-called "end of days," marks the end of the "protective" womb of the patriarchy and the consciousness of victimhood which has grown out of it. It is not the literal "end of the world." It is the ending of a very dysfunctional cycle of human consciousness which coincides with a natural cycle of rapid earth changes, as predicted by the Mayans so long ago, enhanced, no doubt, by mankind's tinkering with the environment in ways we do not even begin to comprehend.

We have actually been going through this shift for all of the 21st century. In large measure, it is a shift that is responsible for much of the stress and pressure we are experiencing in the world. Life is forcing us to birth ourselves into a new adventure where each of us must create and hold up our own life as we have dreamed it throughout eternity. At the same time as a new consciousness is being birthed into the world, we are actually going through the birth canal, ourselves. We are literally giving birth to our new selves as we are asked to birth a new awareness of light and compassion and understanding into the world. And, as any woman who has ever given birth can tell you, the process of giving birth is extremely difficult. It is filled with struggle, pain, even fear, for you really don't know what to expect until it happens.

Because we are alive today, we are the ones who are giving birth to this new consciousness, with all the struggle and sacrifice that a birthing entails. It is a consciousness of Oneness with the

Great Spirit and harmony with all of life, replacing the old consciousness of separation, victimhood and warfare that has plagued us for so long. The Great Dreamer God who has dreamed our dreams for us in so many ways—who among us would ever create for ourselves the dream of such massive suffering and destruction that we have seen through the last hundreds of years?—this Great Dreamer God is waking up. He will no longer be dreaming our dreams for us, thank you very much.

Instead, we each have to take responsibility for our own dreams. The new consciousness which is upon us is a consciousness that says, "I am responsible. I am responsible for what I do and what I do not do in life." It replaces the old consciousness of victimhood and selfishness that says, "Take care of me, regardless of the cost to the world around me."

The good news is that we are not alone in our struggle. The goddess is returning to this world, the sacred feminine consciousness which balances the male consciousness so that there can be true harmony. Harmony is found only where there is balance. There has been an enormous imbalance in the masculine and feminine energies of humankind for many thousands of years, to the point where the sacred feminine was in danger of going out of our lives forever. Think about it, without the mating of the male and the female there can be no life, at all. Where that mating is forced, disharmony and conflict follow. But where the mating is the result of the sacred masculine and the sacred feminine meeting in the center, freely and with joy, a great creativity is born.

This is the new world into which I see us moving. This is what "2012" means to me. It is a new world born of the ancient understanding that all of life is rooted in our Oneness with the great God beings of our existence, born of the ancient understanding and the certainty that we are part of the Great Spirit, just as the Great Spirit is part of each of us. Through our Oneness with God, we are One with all of existence, no longer separated into warring factions.

It is the same understanding and light in which the Ancient Ones walked, magnified a thousand-fold by the great flowering of human ingenuity and creativity that has taken place in the intervening millenniums.

It is my belief in the immense possibilities for good and higher consciousness that has given birth to this book. *Coming Full Circle, Ancient Teachings for a Modern World* is born of my decades of working and growing within the teachings of the Sisterhood of the Shields, as we have sought to apply them to the modern world. It is a book that is intended to help you discover how to elevate yourself, how to elevate your body, mind and spirit to the highest degree possible, beyond anything you ever imagined.

In the process, it is my great pleasure to introduce you to members of this amazing group of women for the very first time and share with you more of our experiences together. Each chapter is about a woman of the Sisterhood of the Shields. Each is accompanied by an article I have written to show you how I translate my experience of these women and their teachings to guide me through my life in our complicated modern world. I hope they will also guide you to a greater understanding and acceptance of the gifts which surround you and are already within you as, together, we find our way through our world.

1

AGNES WHISTLING ELK
The One Who Knows How

THE PRAIRIE GRASS WAS blowing golden and fragrant in rivers of wind. I remembered the clamor of voices in the restaurants of Santa Fe, the shiny faces smiling, voices telling me of so many things. We so want to be appreciated and loved, all of us, but we don't admit our frailties. We hold them against ourselves and think we are, perhaps, unworthy because of them.

I feel these pains so deeply, I thought for a moment, drifting far away.

Agnes Whistling Elk and I were riding across a wilderness grassland. We were laughing like children, galloping over the hills next to each other, our horses frisky, each wanting to stride into the lead. Faster and faster we went, until a stream came into view in a gully up ahead.

We slowed and followed a deer trail down to the edge of a crystal clear stream. My Arabian mare threw her head in anticipation and almost pulled the reins out of my hand as she lowered her head to drink the cool water. To the horses, water was an invitation for life and they drank for several moments.

After dismounting, Agnes pulled her horse's sweet, big-eyed face toward her as she uncinched her saddle and swung it to the ground, placing her saddle blanket on top of it to air. Then she slipped off her gelding's bridle and placed it over the saddle. She scratched the horse's ears and bridle path and kissed his neck as she patted him gently.

"Do as I do," Agnes said, looking at me with a secret smile.

I laughed, remembering those words from so many years ago, when Ruby was testing my commitment by asking me to skin a deer just as she was doing. It was horrifying for me but I did it anyway because I knew I was being tested. Unexpectedly, tears welled up in my eyes as I loosened my saddle and swung it off Maggie's back. I scratched her withers and put my arms around her for a moment. This mare had been through so much with me. The sweet smell of her mane pleased me so.

Agnes cocked her head and watched me like a curious pup, wondering at my tears. I removed Maggie's bridle and the two horses went to the center of the stream and rolled over in the water, scratching their backs and playing.

"It's time, Agnes. It's like this creek water. It's the flow of life. I'm so aware of the beauty and art in life, but the light that illuminates us and creates such power is also what eventually turns us to dust . . . is our destruction."

"Art in life?" Agnes asked.

"I recently saw a documentary on the British sculptor Andy Goldworthy. He has created beautiful sculptures by welding together icicles. With the light and heat of the sun, they come to life, radiant and full of colors. The light that illuminates them also melts them, which I thought was so inspiring."

"Maybe," Agnes said, making herself comfortable on a flat piece of reddish soap stone. "You said something about time and flow. It's not time you feel as much as loss. The world as you know it is being taken from you, you think!" She held up her canteen. "You see the front of this canteen?"

"Yes."

Then she turned it around.

"Now you see the back."

"Yes."

"Is the front still there?"

"You can't see it, but it still exists."

"So just because you can't see it does not mean it is not there. The back cannot exist without the front."

"But . . . ."

"But, you have to learn to see differently."

"But it's solid. I can't see through it," I said mournfully.

"You need to see the whole of things instead of just the parts." She handed me the canteen. I felt it, front and back.

"What's in your hands?" Agnes asked. "Describe it to me."

"Well, it's a canteen that has depth. It's strong and molded and slightly heavy, four-sided. I can hear the water in it."

"How do you know that it has water inside?"

"I feel it sloshing, and I can hear its familiar sound."

"Water?" she asked.

"Water," I stated, feeling silly.

"What is water like?"

"It is clear and fluid and fills whatever vessel it's in. It becomes the form or shape and is changeable."

Agnes watched the horses, who were grazing sleepily.

"Is water something like spirit?" she asked, not looking at me.

"Yes, I guess it is."

"So, there's this container, then, that you can see and not see, filled with something that flows. Let's see. Let's take the canteen," she said, "and empty it into the creek."

Agnes emptied the canteen into the creek.

"See how the water flows into the moving water of the creek? And now, I can fill up the canteen again."

She leaned down and placed the canteen into the creek, refilling it with water. She held up the canteen.

"New water, old canteen. Seen and unseen. Formed and changeable," she said. "What's the word, the feeling that is really causing you such sorrow?"

We sat for a long time watching the creek and the horses as they lay down in the grass to doze.

"I want this moment, like water, to be held in the canteen forever," I said, ignoring her question.

"But then it would become brackish and useless," Agnes countered.

"Maybe I don't want to be useful anymore."

"What isn't useful?" she asked.

"No," I said, thinking of her earlier question about sadness. "It's certitude, isn't it? I get so tired of stepping into the unknown with one person after another. As human beings, we want to be sure things feel secure. When we step into the unknown, we are no longer certain and that frightens us. Oftentimes, it ruins people's lives because they won't step into the unknown and give life a chance. Agnes, there is nothing about what I do that will ever feel secure. Sometimes in my work I forget how vital and vibrant the unknown can be. Then you show me a simple canteen filled with water. I can turn the canteen and see both front and back. I cannot see both sides at the same time, but I know they are there. Then I can drink the water and, like spirit, it becomes part of my form. Unlike the water or the canteen, I really can perceive the wholeness of things as they actually are."

"That's the trick!" Agnes laughed as she got up off the ground.

We began to saddle our horses. They were anxious to head for home and dinner.

"As we really are," she said as we mounted and headed back through the sea of grass. "Trust in your perception, Lynn. That's the secret!"

We laughed as we rode toward home at a gentle cantor, the canteen swinging over my shoulder.

It is at times like these that I truly appreciate how far I have come with these magnificent women. I was their apprentice for so many years, and then I became a member of the Sisterhood, but I still have so much to learn from them. They were born to a tradition and a spirituality that has been carried in their blood-lines and practiced by their ancestors for millenniums. And while they remind me often that I, also, have had many lifetimes in many different traditions, I also have lifetimes of catching up to do. Our lives and our memories have been so different for many centuries.

At moments like these, however, I also realize how much we have grown together in this lifetime. When I first met and began working with them, I was hugely intimidated, as well as being in total awe of them. There were many who seemed to hold me at arm's length, whether out of respect for my relationship as Agnes's apprentice or because I came from such a different world, I don't know.

What I am sure of is that it was an honor beyond compare to be initiated into their circle as a full member, standing shoulder-to-shoulder with one another, each of us equidistant from the center which is the Great Spirit and the Oneness of all of life. In many ways, I am still their student and I have much to learn, but we are also friends who grow and learn from each other, sharing our very different world views in the way that only friends can.

We have, indeed, come full circle.

Circling Back: "Life, A Glorious Rite of Passage"

If you believe that life is sacred, then you begin to realize that you have a sense of mission, a sense of purpose in your life. This sense of purpose is what makes you search for what is true and real for you.

It is so difficult for modern people to find what is true and real for us. We live in a world that has largely lost its sense of mission, other than to have its own way, even when we don't really know what that 'way' is and regardless of the consequences. When the primary focus of your life is to have your own way, you are destined to a life of frustration and confusion, at best.

It hasn't always been this way. People the world over have long sought a sense of the meaning of life, a search that has dominated the development of religious, philosophical and political thought for ages. For most of this same time, however, indigenous peoples never lost their sense of purpose in life, although, tragically, that is changing as the constraints of modern living increasingly intrude on them.

Throughout much of their history, native peoples have understood their sense of purpose by celebrating their connection between their own lives and the lives of their ancestors and the gods and goddesses of their existence through carefully constructed rites of passage: rituals and ceremonies guided by the wisdom and advice of the elders and the elders' elders which grow out of their collective and individual spiritual understanding of the universe. These are ceremonies designed to inform and prepare the people, as spiritual initiates, for the road that lies ahead.

Western cultures tend to look at rites of passage as quaint, marking mostly the passages into puberty, adulthood or old age and not really relevant in our "advanced" way of living. One of the rites of passage we actually do celebrate—marriage—has come to be more centered around the bride's wedding gown than what a marriage represents in the life of the community and the lives of those who enter into it.

In contrast, Zoila, a teacher from the Yucatán and member of the Sisterhood, took me through an ancient and very intense Mayan rite of passage which was held for young women about to give birth. It was a rite of passage that marked the end of their lives as girls and the beginning of their lives as women with responsibility for others, and it gave them a deeply probative examination into the innate differences between people and how to guide their own family dynamics through these confusing waters. It was about teaching young women a new, age-appropriate understanding of the world into which they were stepping and how to find their place in it without losing themselves or their loved ones.

What a rite of passage is, in actuality, is the celebration of facing a major milestone in your life, one that is age-related or perhaps one that grows out of a profound shift in your circumstances, by welcoming the challenge it gives you to grow into the best person you can be. Whether it is a serious, life-altering experience or the passage from one stage of life to another, if you look at what you are facing it and celebrate it as an opportunity to grow into a new level of awareness, open yourself to the wisdom this change brings, you will find that you experience far less confusion in your daily life. You can create your own celebrations to mark your trail through life or you can learn about and observe traditional celebrations. Either way, observing rites of passage as you face life's challenges is a way of learning how to take responsibility for your life and celebrating yourself as you seek to understand where you have been and where you are going next.

Some people don't want to acknowledge any of the passages in their lives, don't want to get older in wise blood, or even move from adolescence into adulthood. Many people are not thrilled about taking responsibility for what they create and what their life is becoming. We live in a blame society where the other guy is always wrong, where everything that needs fixing is someone else's responsibility, and where far too many people simply don't want to be personally accountable.

I would like to challenge this way of living right now. I consider being born into this lifetime as its own rite of passage in respect to our larger process of enlightenment. If you could, imagine just for a moment that you sit with the Creator Gods before you are born. You sit with them and you look at your spirit shield, the beautiful manifestation of your spirit as it spins with you from lifetime to lifetime. You sit with them and look at how this shield has been imprinted with the experiences of various lifetimes. Then, as you look toward the life you are about to enter, the Creator Gods help you to see that there are aspects of your own enlightenment that you have not yet dealt with, things you need to face in order to become enlightened.

What might you become in this crazy world of ours if you were to look at your entire life in this way, looking for what is missing from your understanding of life and celebrating and welcoming the challenge to become the most illumined person you can possibly be? Then, when you look at the circumstances into which you were born, whether it was into an abusive family, into wealth or into poverty, and when you look at the situations that you have faced in your life, the difficult and emotional passages you have gone through, you find that they were part of a continuum of learning what you need to learn about living. You might even discover that there are lessons that you have not yet learned in this lifetime and look forward to the opportunity to learn them.

What might your life become if you were to stop fighting what you came here to learn in the first place and instead celebrated and welcomed it? Then you truly begin to see that the life you live is about the choices you make. You always have choices. You can choose to look at the struggles you face today, which people the world over are facing at this point in human history, as miseries to be endured. Or you can choose to look at them as the challenge to celebrate your ability to elevate yourself to a higher level of being. Either way, the conflicts and problems we face are not going to go away until we—individually and collectively—take responsibility for them.

When I work with people who have had great difficulty in life, who have come to me seeking not to lament their plight and receive pity, but rather to find out where they can make changes and change the direction of their lives, I find that these people have probably experienced their entire lives as a rite of passage. I don't believe that the great Creator Beings, the prime movers, God in whatever way you understand the source of life, would ever give you something more than you can handle.

It's important to see that life truly is a celebration of passages. And yes, there really are very specific ceremonies for different stages of your physical existence that can help you to move through them in enlightened, life-affirming ways. Living this way means, however, that you have to take responsibility for the choices you have made. Even though it may have felt more like a dictate than a choice at the time, everything you have done has been a matter of choice.

You also take responsibility for the places where you are most fragile. You take responsibility for discovering and learning what it is you don't know, that is standing in your way. There is something about modern societies that teaches us to cover up our frailties, teaches that vulnerability is a fault and a sign of weakness instead of a mirror of our own pathway towards enlightenment. Honoring a rite of passage means accepting *with a sacred purpose* your vulnerabilities as very important and essential places of learning within your soul. What could be more worthwhile, really?

Rites of passage celebrate the differences as well as the similarities that we all have. They make us see how precious, how beautiful and how unique each one of us truly is. Through rites of passage, you see the totality of your life, not just a series of isolated incidents. There is a beauty, a balance, a power within each of us, but so few of us seem to know how to access that aesthetic and present it into our lives as part of our wholeness. Rites of passage are about health; they are about balance between the physical and the spiritual you.

When you acknowledge the experiences of your life and welcome the challenges, you go deeply into your psyche and your emotions so that you can let go of old baggage that no longer serves you. You move into new aspects of creativity and freedom that are your rewards for conscious living.

You learn to resonate with the rhythms of nature. Pieces of confusion drop away as you begin to celebrate who you are, not just who the world wants you to be. All your life, you have had a sense that there is a knowing within your own being, but you don't always know how to welcome that knowing. Rites of passage connect you with it in a conscious way. They are about finding the heartland within your own spirit, that place that is magical and free and full of a kind of wildness, an instinctual nature that can express itself without guilt or fear.

Wisdom really only becomes part of your personal domain through some aspect of experience. By marking the milestones of your journeys in life, you arrive at new positions of power, balance and understanding. You are able to see clearly who you are and how proud you can be of all that you have accomplished, even if it may have seemed insignificant at the time.

Rites of passage aren't some quaint window into the lives of distant and far-removed worlds. They are a vibrant way of living life today to its fullest, most glorious extent.

Celebrate your life, don't hide it. When you go through hardship, understand that it is but a passage from one level of your existence to a higher level if that is what you choose to make it. Whether you are going through the age-related phases of your life or guiding your children and friends through them, celebrate them as the true rites of passage that they are, a bridge between where you have been and where you are going next. We rarely hold our elders in esteem in our world, allowing them to show us the way just as their elders showed it to them. Still, their wisdom is there, anywhere you care to look. There are so many resources available to us today, there is simply no longer any excuse for ignorance of any aspect of our lives. Seek out the voices of those who have already walked the trail you are on and celebrate with them the passages of your life. Share your learning and your growth with your family and friends. In doing so, you will find a richness of life of which you have perhaps only dreamed.

2

WINONA

WE HAD BEEN SITTING together for some time under a graceful old palm tree at the edge of a placid Hawaiian sea. The hydrangea bushes behind us formed a dense pattern of thick green with huge pink flowers. Warm trade winds blew in from the west, carrying the scent of the sea as they caressed our skin, gently, like spun silk.

Clouds were misting down over the mountains. The volcanoes, now dormant, were green, with *kukui* grass growing over the hardened lava flows. The edges of the lava, rough and jagged, reminded me of the legends of the fiery Hawaiian goddess Pele, "She Who Shapes the Sacred Land," and her flight from her enraged sister Namakaokaha'i after Pele seduced her husband. According to legend, Pele fled to the Big Island's Mauna Loa Volcano, the tallest mountain in the world. She now resides in the Big Island's Kilauea Volcano and spews forth molten lava flows as she continues to create new land. Her sister, Namakaokaha'i, lives on the island of Kauai.

"You calculate what you see and experience," Winona said to me, breaking into my reverie. Her expression was sly as she fiddled with the white plumeria blossoms fastened in her thick, long gray hair.

"I am not calculating," I said, indignant.

"Calculating is an aspect of control, before you act. That is the warrior's way, and you are a hunter." She thought for a moment, watching the water folding in over the sand.

"The tide rhythms are so powerful," I said.

"Is that tide an aspect of Mother Nature's decision, or is it a force of letting go?" Win asked me.

I smoothed the white sand with my fingers, feeling the power of the volcanic earth breathing beneath us.

"It feels like an inhale and an exhale, but I'm not aware of a decision being made by life force, maybe just a letting go."

"Yes," Winona said, circling her arms around us both. Her arms were tattooed in Polynesian designs, as were her legs, making her appearance strong and somewhat ferocious. "No one can shove you if you're a warrior of spirit," she said, giving me a push. She laughed gently, as if to say, *'Pay attention.'*

"You are not being blown around like sand in the wind, but I can still push you a little because you are of this time and of this soil. You would never do anything against yourself. You are a survivor beyond your knowing. You have changed the flow of your own karma because you have perfect pitch, or attunement, that never misses a beat."

Winona had so engulfed me with her presence that I simply stared in amazement at her exquisite, primitive beauty.

"Thank you." I hesitated. "I want to get beautiful tattoos, live by the sea and know you, understand you."

"Oh, yes, and ride the dolphins!" She laughed, making her belly jiggle under her *pareo*. "But you can only know me as power. Our early life was so different. A warrior is the sum of her aspects of personal power, and that determines how we experience each other. Remember, no one can make you do something against your own judgment. There is a force in you that is like the tides, that you can read. It's a kind of abandonment."

Winona took a pinch of tobacco and offered it to the spirit of the wind.

"Come. The tide is coming in like your true nature, and no force can stop it. We are done here."

She extended her hand and pulled me to my feet. A surge of seawater surrounded us suddenly, washing our feet. Shortly thereafter, I was driving us toward Havi, a small village to the north, a more rainy area of the island where Winona's home over-looked the sea from dense, jungle-like growth.

"I wonder at my own life, teaching about the wonders of consciousness," I said to her. She put her hand on my shoulder.

"Little Wolf, you teach as you have in so many lifetimes, and it makes you feel isolated and alone much of the time."

"It's true," I said to her, trying to remember what it was like when I didn't teach and write, when I was just living an ordinary life.

"Ah, your life has never been ordinary," she said to my thoughts. "Think of the turtles," she added, taking out a crayon and tearing off a piece of a paper bag she had gotten from the grocery store. She drew a turtle with many squares on the back of its shell.

"This life is like pieces of a puzzle. We fit these pieces together, one by one. Childhood, adolescence, the seasons of life, adulthood, the knowing so much and our bodies getting closer and closer to Mother Earth as we grow older." Winona began to laugh, barely audible, with a sweeping smile crossing her face.

"We are like the shell of the great sea turtle. We carry on our backs our history and the history of our people, but that history is only that. It does not fill you with sadness because you realize it is part of the dream."

"I know that, but still, it is a predatory universe. Sometimes I can hardly bear it, our treatment of animals, for instance."

Winona shook her head. "When you say that, I see your aura draw close to your body, as if you are protecting yourself from pain. When you take your aura and hold it close to you because of your emotions, because of fear or anger, you lose the brilliance and luminosity of your light body," she said.

"How is our astral body different from our light body? Or is it?"

"For humans, we have many levels of light bodies explained by different religions and texts in many different ways. As I see it," she said, holding her hands out in front of herself as if touching a beautiful fabric with her fingers, "your astral body is part of your emotions. Your emotions live in the west on the sacred wheel. It is, perhaps, your most female lodge. It is receptive and feels everything you perceive.

"In the east lives your mind, your rational self. That is a different lodge altogether, filled with rational energy, a discerning energy. But your emotions and moisture create the astral field. They create changes of light, depending on which chakra, or energy center, you are living in. If you're centered mostly in the root chakra, full of anger, then your astral field will be tinged with red, moving up into orange and perhaps into gold, which is your sacred will, all having to do with how you express what you feel.

"Then you move from the astral into the etheric field. By the way, first attention is your ordinary life in the physical world. Second attention moves into the astral, and third attention is in the etheric world. The etheric levels of consciousness are the places where higher consciousness dwells. This higher consciousness is sometimes used by scientists or highly evolved mathematicians, like Einstein, who could tune into that higher frequency of consciousness and receive answers. The problem for them, and for all human beings, is that we receive these notes of wisdom through our own instruments, and our instruments can be distorted and have failings, flaws. In that respect, you might not be able to translate the wisdom that comes to you. That is a possibility."

Winona was leaning forward and tapping softly on the dashboard, like a drum, as I drove.

I brushed the hair out of my eyes. The sky was growing ever more blue after days of rain, which had washed the trees and leaves. The shininess of the earth was startling. The sea was a peaceful blue, dark and deep. Winona gave me a couple of macadamia nuts from her bag. I remained silent.

"Symbolically," she continued, "the turtle carries Mother Earth on her back. Mother Earth is symbolized by the turtle in many great pathways around the world. She is slow-moving, protected, and enormously wise with her memories of lifetimes and millenniums in her soul."

I took a deep breath, imagining the beauty of the creative mind.

"Is it possible to move into someone else's mind and move their consciousness," I asked, "give them an idea that would change their life somehow? Is that possible?"

Winona looked at me and then looked away, out the window, at the passing volcanic wedges.

"You can change how someone thinks. I suppose that if you were intent on such an endeavor, you would move into a place that we call the 'dream within the dream.'"

"I don't understand," I said. "I know there's dreaming and flying in my dreams, because I visit you all the time and love being in Hawaii, flying over the volcanic mountains and the sea. But I don't really understand the 'dream within the dream.' Would you tell me the way you see that?"

"There is regular dreaming, when you go to sleep and have a dream. There is also lucid dreaming, which means that through the process of will you can go into other dream dimensions,

dimensions that are unknown to us in the physical world but which are as real as the physical world. When you 'dream within the dream,' you are sound asleep in a regular dream and at the same time, you know that you are dreaming, that you can go to a different level in the dream if that is your intent. You become conscious that you are dreaming, but you do not wake up. Instead, you move even deeper within the dream. For example, let's say that in your dream you are going to the Library of Alexandria, in ancient times. Then you change your mind. You decide to go to Socrates, instead, and you change the direction of the dream. You don't do this with your conscious mind, because you are physically asleep. You do it with your dream body, that part of you that dreams, that part of you that is a bridge between the conscious mind and the subconscious mind."

With her red crayon, Winona drew a picture of a sea turtle on a paper bag. She pointed to the turtle and said, "See all these squares that are on the turtle's back? They are all different conscious relationships on this earth. Language creates the society in which you live. Society creates a certain consciousness. So these squares are about language and society and belief structures, like religions and the fighting and stupidity." She poked her crayon through the paper in a moment of frustration. "Why can we not lift this whole world up into higher consciousness?"

"Why is it that with all that we know, we cannot somehow help people to see the paradise that our human life could be, the power that we have in the mind when we use it properly?" I asked.

"Yes," said Winona. "The power is what most people don't see. They don't understand that we really create our own reality. We've created our bodies, we've created our experiences, and we can create new experience in the future."

"But that takes on karma, does it not? I can't imagine that."

"Well, yes, of course it takes on karma. However, maybe it's all just a dream."

"If it really is a dream," I asked her, "can there be karma in the dream, do you think, in a certain way?"

"What do you think?" Winona said to me, her eyes sparkling.

"Yes," I said, answering my own question. "But I am so exhausted. I don't know how to teach people, anymore," I said, shaking my head.

"That's why we pray," Winona said. "What's why we pray endlessly. But we don't have much time, now."

"What do you mean?" I asked.

"The end of the calendars means something. My ancient family was part of the astrology-makers of that world. They understood the stars. There is a great cross in the Milky Way, called by the Mayans the 'Crossroads.' In 2012, the alignment between the December solstice sun and the Crossroads area of the Milky Way will be powerful and can create destruction. We want the wisdom of my ancestors. We need it, but others destroyed much of it long ago. There are pieces, keys that we can no longer find from the ancient Mayan world, the Olmec world. What's left to us is what they wrote about the *end* of the calendar, but there are keys that are missing both before and after that 'end'."

"Well," I said, "I'm convinced that the key we need is the use of thought, like that square right there." I reached over and pointed to a particular square she had drawn on the turtle. "Right up there, at the top, at the base of the head. To me, that is where the 'dream within the dream' is. I think that the danger comes in when uninformed people begin to understand that you can dream within the dream, that there is something before creation. Perhaps some would misuse that thought power to take for themselves and destroy the rest of the world."

"That is the issue," Winona said. "That's why the Sisterhood doesn't have anybody else out there teaching, except you."

"Thanks a lot!" I said. "I could use some help, you know."

Winona laughed, patting me on my arm. "Look, Lynn, you are doing the most wonderful job. Don't be concerned that you aren't doing enough, because you couldn't do more. Dreaming within the dream is another story, and you know it. You've been there."

"Yes, I have," I said, "but it's hard to know where the boundaries are in the dream. I can dream. I can move around in this world, and I can disguise myself. Probably nobody knows that I have a dream body. And playing the fool is just fine with me. But you and I are talking about what we consider to be somewhat real. I want to understand the bridge between the conscious and subconscious mind."

We pulled up in front of Winona's house. As we carried our groceries into her wooden-planked house to put them away, a little mama pig and her babies ran by the front door. It was a simple, pristinely clean home neatly nestled among large, leafy trees. Going back outside, we sat on her whitewashed porch and watched the piglets for a few minutes, before they got scared away.

"I feed them from time to time," she said, "so they aren't terribly afraid of us. But they are destructive because they do eat everything in sight. But it's okay, because I can just replant. I put little fences around the plants I don't want them to have."

I watched the sky. Heavy clouds were coming in from the west. The trade winds were beginning to blow a little harder and the sweet smell of earth and jungle foliage and flowers scented the air. We got up and went back into the house. The inside of her house was fresh, the walls a very pale yellow. A small wind chime by the window tinkled in the background, a beautiful, gentle sound.

"I always feel hopeful when I see yellow, particularly on walls," I told her.

She smiled and said, "Yes, the color makes me feel good, too."

Helping her put the groceries away, I turned around and saw the far end of her living room and realized that nearly the whole wall was covered in a beautiful painting. It reminded me of Monet, splashes of color, magnificent golds and blues depicting a beautiful scene of the sunset over mountains and ocean, with a small hut set at the side of a pond which reflected the mountains around it. It was a very Hawaiian setting, peaceful and magnificently executed. I was transfixed by the picture and walked into the living room.

Presently, Winona came in from the kitchen and said, "I painted this painting. It is a shaman painting, a painting from the sacred people of Hawaii, in honor of them."

I traced the colors in my mind, the configurations. Finally, I said, "I love art. I have followed art and great painters all of my life. My mother would read me stories of the lives of artists and composers when I was a little girl as I was falling asleep. I remember the story of Picasso. It was very interesting to me. He was quite a genius in his time, but I've never really been able to relate to his paintings."

Winona looked at me with a smile and grabbed a piece of what looked like butcher paper and some crayons. She sat down on the wooden floor and began drawing cubes, filling them with different colors. She drew cubes and angular settings and a figure near a pond, similar to the painting I was looking at on her wall except that the cubes appeared, to me, devoid of any beauty. A bit of time went by as she filled in the cubes and the geometric designs. Finally, she looked up at me, pulling back the hair that was falling into her face and getting in her way. She tied it with a rubber band from her pocket.

"You know, these cubical drawings are like Picasso, but different paintings are different from one another because of the painter," she said.

I thought about it for a while and asked, "You are familiar with Zen painting, yes?"

"From Japan, you mean? I love the work. The thing I notice most about them is that the Zen painters always make their human beings very small and nature very large," she said.

"Yes, yes!," I said excitedly. "It's true, because nature is our greatest teacher. Nature is what makes those pen and ink drawings, those brush strokes of the Zen so powerful, just a few lines that convey so much expression." The women of the Sisterhood live essentially without the modern amenities which we so take for granted, and I am always surprised by how truly worldly their knowledge and vision are. I never know when they already know what I am talking about and when I am introducing them to something new.

"You know, Lynn, here's a drawing," she said pointing to the cubicals she had been tracing on the paper. "What do you think is the difference between these and the painting I did on the wall?"

"Well," I said, "there is much difference. The feeling is different, the color is different."

Winona asked me, "What does color say to you?"

"The splashes of the misty palette on your wall speak to me of serenity," I answered.

"Come, come. You know what I am talking about."

Finally I said, "It's soul, isn't it? Spirit. To me, there is no soul in these cubist pictures, although there are some Picasso's that I really love, but not many. His partner for many long years, Françoise Gilot, was someone whom I met and admired hugely. I read her book, *My Life With Picasso*."

By now, I was sitting on the floor, looking at Winona's painting and tracing the lines with my fingers.

"Françoise did some interesting paintings. She called them 'Shamanic Wandering' paintings. I bought a couple of them. They were of the elementals. As I look at your painting, I can see that her vision was as a bridge between the kind of shaman painting that you made on your wall, Winona, and the cubistic style that you are showing on the butcher paper."

"The teachers like Klee and Picasso and so many of that ilk were scientists," I continued. "They were not shamans, teachers of wisdom, whatever you want to call us. I've never quite been able to figure out what we are, but shamans we certainly are and we live the world of mysticism."

She said, "Exactly, we live in the world of soul."

She got up and got us lemonade from the refrigerator. Even the glass tasted good, and the ice against my lips. I took a deep breath and leaned up against the wall so that I could absorb more of her painting, feel the essence of it.

I felt the stillness in it and said to her, "You live in the most beautiful place in the world. The peace, the serenity, the trade winds, the sunlight, the rain, the temperate climate, all of it is what I love. You are an extraordinary teacher, Winona, and I appreciate it so." I gestured toward her wall. "I have never seen anything like this before. I have been around art my whole life, loved it and studied it and even sold it as an art representative. During all of that time, I never realized how much the native people paint from a place of passion. You paint of your lives, the spirits that animate you and your lives, whatever it is you are doing, perhaps hunting. It is always the beauty of spirit beings, like the Hopi *kachina* dolls. Those are very interesting."

"Ah, yes," she said and she pulled me by the hand into the other room, where she had a whole shelf filled with *kachina* dolls from the Hopi and Zuni, Pueblo Indian art.

"Sit down just a minute." She tugged on my arm. "Sit on the floor with me and look at these beings. If you close your eyes just a little, you will begin to see them dance before you. They are dancers. They are the essence of a form."

I studied them through nearly closed eyes. "Yes. They are so beautiful and I have loved them always. I wish I knew more about them."

She said, "Well, you don't need to know more about them except that a good artist portrays the spirit of a thunder being, for example, in a way that can be understood by anyone who looks at it."

"What do you mean, exactly?" I asked.

"Well, think about it this way. Take mush that is cooking on the stove. When it starts to cook and get very, very hot, steam starts rising out of it. These *kachinas* are like the steam from the mush, they are the essence of the mush, not the mush, itself. They are not the form of the mush, they are the essence of it. That's what spirit dolls are about. If you have a wolf *kachina*, it is the spirit or the essence of the wolf, but not the wolf itself," she said.

"Your painting," I finally said, "is the essence of you and the beauty and the magic you are."

We took our lemonade and went back through the other room, to sit on the porch and watch the sun set through the trees, into the ocean below.

Circling Back: "The Power of Spiritual Integrity"

In beauty is truth. In this simple statement is found all the power that you will ever need in life. Find what is beautiful for you and you will find your truth. Find your truth and you will find your power. Winona is an excellent example of this. She is a shaman woman of formidable powers, powers which are born of her deep love of the beauty of the natural world. She had painted this world on her walls, "To honor the sacred people of the land," she said.

In the Hawaiian language, there is a word for the magical world where the sacred souls of the people meet the majesty of nature. That word is *Aina*.

Hawaiians have a spirituality that is built upon a reverence for their ancestors. They believe that their ancestors control the elements of nature, like wind and rain, and send them vital messages through the elements to guide them on their journeys through life. To them, the natural world is sacred. When it rains, they believe that the rain is a message from the ancestors to remind them of something they have forgotten, depending on what kind of rain it is, and there are many different words for 'rain' in their language.

Throughout the world of shamanism, from Hawai'i to Siberia, from Manitoba to South America, Africa and Australia, wherever in the physical world it is practiced and in whatever form, the natural world is sacred. Shamanic peoples would never violate Mother Earth in the ways which modern cultures do.

To me, shamanism is a powerful and beautiful world view, born of the interconnectedness of all living things in the universe, both seen and unseen. What an exquisite way to know sacredness, that we are all part of the great One and that the Oneness of life flows through all living things, plant and animal alike, the winds, the seas, the rains, the world of spirit world and the world of the physical, even other universes, connecting all that is in the great dance we humans call life.

When I speak of finding your power in life, I am not talking of power over anyone else. I am talking about the power of the integrity of your own spirit, a power which is awakened by beauty. It is the greatest power you can ever develop, born as it is from the love of the Great Spirit. Then you can accomplish anything that you set your mind and your heart to accomplish.

Many years ago, I was down in the jungles of the Yucatán working with Zoila Gutierez, a shaman healer of Mayan descent. She is an elderly woman of tremendous physical presence and power. The first time I ever met her, I could see a coiled serpent behind her eyes, which were kind and gentle, and I knew that I would never cross her. Yet her grandchildren ran in and out of the yard with gleeful abandon, interrupting us and asking to be told one story after another. They were completely confident being their own exuberant, laughing selves with her.

I learned much from this woman, even as she challenged and confronted me with some of the most arduous and terrifying physical ordeals I have ever faced. One of the most important things she taught me was how to listen from my heart.

In some respects, I have always experienced life from my heart. My father was an angry man, often slipping beyond anger into pure rage, and the doors to my soul, to my feelings, to my heart, would close. As young as the age of five, I used to climb high up in the apple trees and sit for hours, writing to open those doors.

My parents were very artistic people and I have been surrounded by beautiful works of art throughout my entire life. I even learned how to play the piano as a young child. In art, in whatever form it is created, I have always found an expression of the human soul that can transform my point of view from one of desperation to one of total bliss in the blink of an eye.

Nature, when we experience the majesty and the beauty in her, has this same ability. I remember the first time I met Zoila. As we were speaking in her garden, an exquisite iridescent green hummingbird flew between us and explored a fuchsia bush. Zoila nodded toward it and told me to, "Watch how the hummingbird uses power." The hummingbird hovered in front of the flower, sensing whether its pollen was right. Pollen is power to this bird, a tiny bird that is, itself, so powerful that some migrate a few thousand miles each spring and fall.

"Listen with your heart," Zoila said to me. "Listen with your heart and you will always know when the timing is right, just like the hummingbird. It listens with all of its senses. When the hummingbird senses the timing is right, it joins with the flower. It takes what it needs and nothing more. It does not violate the flower or its spirit. It takes what it needs as it deposits new fertile pollen in return, and then it flies away."

I realize, upon reflection, that this is what happens to me when I am in the presence of art that is great for me. I stand before it and listen with my heart until just the right moment; then I join with it. My heart swells, and I begin to glow within from an inner radiance. That inner radiance comes from the place of virtue within me, the place where I find inner truth.

Virtue is one of the passive qualities of power. In our world, we are so often inculcated to see passivity as an undesirable trait, somehow wimpy and lacking in courage. In reality, passivity can be an integral aspect of great power, as when we sit in total stillness and allow the bedlam of life to go on around us while we focus on connecting with our inner voice of truth. It takes enormous personal strength to be able to do this. Passivity allows us to access the inner voice that tells us what is right and what is not right in any given situation, as opposed to reacting out of fear, greed or judgment.

Virtue is the place of illumination within us. As that radiance grows within you, it becomes integrity. For me, art is the pollen that awakens the spirit of virtue that becomes spiritual integrity. I do not take the artwork away with me. I take the virtue that it awakens within me, which, in turn, empowers my own spirit and life.

The same thing happens with all forms of beautiful art, whether it is the magic and artistry of nature, paintings, photography, poetry, literature, dance, song. Beauty awakens the spirits within us and makes our hearts soar.

Art is the language of the soul. It has the ability to raise our frequency, to lift up our spirits until we are in our highest self. When you walk in the world from the place of your highest self, you walk with spiritual integrity.

I don't know that I fully appreciated the transformational power of art until I learned how to listen with my heart that day in the Yucatán with Zoila. And I am so thankful that I did, otherwise I might not have been able to experience Winona's exquisite painting with such depth and clarity. When you listen with your heart, you move to the center of your personal truth in life. This is when you are the most powerful, when you are living your own truth and not someone else's. You are seeing the world through your own eyes, living your own life. There is no greater power in the world than the power of living your own truth.

It is the beauty with which you surround yourself that awakens you to the power of your truth. Spend time every day exploring what is beautiful to you. Visit libraries and museums, music stores, art galleries and the boutiques of your village or city, where artists showcase their wares. Go for long walks somewhere in nature. Watch the magnificence of storm clouds as they gather on the horizon. Become as the hummingbird in search of your own special pollen. When you find it, sit with it until it begins to dance with you, until it awakens you to your personal power, and then mate with that power within you.

This is how you will know the transformational power and beauty of spiritual integrity.

3

PAINTED BIRD

Painted Bird is a colorful woman. She is a member of the Sisterhood of the Shields and I am pleased to introduce her to you here.

Painted Bird comes from the Solala region of Guatemala and has lived all of her life around Lake Atitlán, an area lush, beautiful, and filled with enormous power. The Lake is in a caldera formed by a volcanic eruption over eighty thousand years ago. There are two volcanoes within the caldera and it is flanked by a third in the south. It is believed to be the deepest lake in Central America, although its bottom has never been explored.

Painted Bird is a mirror of Lake Atitlán. When you are in her presence, you feel the power and mystery of the green, volcanic mountain covered with lush grasses, flowers, and trees.

Lake Atitlán, itself, is a lake of beauty and intrigue. Although ringed by Quiché Mayan villages, at the time I was there, there were few roads around it. You traveled by boat or on steep mountain paths. It is a magnificent reflecting lake. Mysterious winds blow across the region, and the Lake has been known to shake and move unpredictably, imperceptible to our eyes but strong enough that someone who is in a canoe or boat can be submerged by a single giant wave. Many people have died because of this. It is a very odd energy.

The villagers have been under the rule of an antagonistic government for many long years, and it has been extremely difficult for shamans to practice. They are only allowed to have a limited number in any gathering. They meet at night in the caves on the mountains. Sometimes, walking on the beach from the little village of Panajachel, you can look up in the distance and see fires in the caves, making the mountain appear to be covered with fireflies. It is magnificent, and you know that something sacred is coming from those fires and from that light.

Painted Bird lives in a little village on the far side of Lake Atitlán. You walk there by trail or go by boat, depending on how you feel about the volcano on a given day. On one such day, I went to the village by boat, keeping to the edges of the lake for a little more safety. She met me at the shore, along with some of the elders of her village. I felt like Mary Magdalene arriving in *La Mer* in France as I stepped out of the boat into sand and lake water up to my waist. Surprised at the depth, I held my woven cotton bag up in the air.

They greeted me with song, elders, little children and Painted Bird, with a live parrot on her shoulder. They gave me a *huipile*, a Central American blouse, in the very special and colorful weavings of their village. Each village has its own weavings with their own meanings. This one had Quetzalcoatl, the sacred bird of Guatemala, woven into its fabric.

Painted Bird was so happy to see me. Along with the *huipile*, she placed a necklace of silver *Milagros* around my neck, *Milagros*, prayers for all the different aspects of my life, prayers for the animals and for the sacred people. I gave these elegant people gifts of food, and to Painted Bird I gave a beautiful turquoise bracelet.

I had only known Painted Bird from meetings of the Sisterhood around the world, and I was so excited. Being with her in her native environment, one might think that she had never traveled out of her village, but in fact she has traveled a great deal.

Her eyes are magnificent deep pools of light and wisdom that remind me of Lake Atitlán. I don't think you could meet her without thinking of the lake. She is very primitive in one sense and worldly in another. As you are gifted to be with her in her own village, you see how much the volcano that she has lived upon her whole life is part of her personality. She will erupt in laughter and flows of emotion. She is very different from most of the other people I have met in that area, strong in her opinions, very strong, like the mountains. The mountain is there, and you are going to adjust to that mountain or she will take you in some way.

Being with Painted Bird is a most interesting and informative experience. It is a quickening just to be in her presence, empowering, inspiring you to be better, more impeccable in your ways.

One evening toward the end of my time there, we talked late into the night. Then I curled up on a hammock stretched from the house to a tree and fell fast asleep. I was awakened in the morning by an unfamiliar slapping sound, and I rolled out of the hammock as quickly as I could. I got up to find Painted Bird working with her backstrap loom, leaning into the belt around her back to tighten the vertical fibers she was threading onto the loom for a new weaving.

She handed me a clay cup of coffee and I said, "Thank you. Good morning!" She was cheerful. She looked up at the sky as if I was very late getting up, which I was. I must have been exhausted.

I went over and touched the hand-made loom. It was beautiful, so useful and so very well-used. It was shiny from the pressure of her hands and her fingers over many weavings.

She showed me the dark purple thread that she was putting on the loom. Then she gestured to shelves holding bowls of berries. "These are the berries," she said, getting up. She picked a berry out of one of the bowls and showed it to me. "These are the berries that we use for this purple color. Don't get it on you, because you can't get it off."

She went back to her weaving. Then she took my fingers and ran them over the threads she had placed on the loom.

"These are your vertical threads, Painted Bird. To me, they are like our lives," I said, reflectively.

Painted Bird thought about that for a minute and she said, "Yes, they are the foundation threads. Then we weave in the colors and symbols with the horizontal threads. The horizontal threads are for the beauty of the weaving. They are for the colors and the light. The purple thread is the background, representing the dark color of blood, the dark power of our structure and who we are as people."

Taking a break from her weaving, she held the loom, which was strapped around her back, with one hand and took my hand with her other, and we walked together to the water's edge. It was beautiful, reflecting the cobalt blue sky of lofty, puffy clouds. The volcano, not far away, seemed to be sleeping. A little cloud around the top of it was so still, like the hat on someone who does mime.

Painted Bird sat down on the sand and patted the ground for me to join her, which I did happily, sipping my coffee, waking up slowly. "You see," she said, picking up a stick and making a circle in the sand. "That is a form."

"Painted Bird, all the women of the Sisterhood seem to be talking to me about form," I said. "We shift that form into light, don't we?"

"Yes!" she said, delighted. "Yes, yes. We have to be so direct and discerning." She used words in Quiché that I did not altogether understand, but I could tell what she meant by her expression, by the way she stabbed the stick into the sand as she said the word for 'discernment.'

She drew a directional cross within the circle and said, "My weaving is within this circle of form. I am creating a form that has a meaning, that has a sacred voice. That is why I use the directional cross of the four sacred directions to guide my weaving. But you can only come to the sacred voice when you totally understand what weaving means."

"Well, you have the vertical threads, the purple threads, right? The background threads, the foundation."

"Yes," she nodded.

"Then the design within the cross is going to be made up of many colors. Is that correct?"

"Yes, but with the perpendicular threads. Without those threads, I could not create the *huipile*," which is what she was making. "Every time you place a vertical thread on a loom, you've got to make absolutely sure that you remember what you're doing. The vertical threads are of the earth. As I weave, the earth is part of creating something that somebody will wear, that somebody may wear for a lifetime and hand down to their children, something that has a meaning."

She studied the many vibrantly colored yarns that were in a basket next to her, waiting to be woven through the loom. "Here, this is a gathering of all of the horizontal yarns," she said. They were strong natural fibers that had been hand-woven and worked into threads.

A high mist was in the air that had come up across the distant mountains. The green of the mountains and the land around us was luscious. It enlivened me as I sat with Painted Bird, whose hair was tied up in a kind of knot. She was wearing a yellow *huipile* and a denim skirt and sandals. She was lovely, and I was so glad to be with her.

She stopped weaving. "You see this cross," she said as she drew a figure in the sand. "Today I need to figure out what is going to bring the most beauty to the person for whom I am weaving this. I always do it that way," she said, laughing. "Not all people are the same, of course." She shrugged and bumped my elbow with hers and laughed. Her explosive laughter was wonderful. Again I looked over to the volcano, wondering if it was about to move, but it seemed very quiet.

"You see these beautiful horizontal threads?" She pulled a beautiful yellow out of the basket. Yellow is one of my favorite colors. To many people, it represents joy and hope, and this day I was filled with hope. Hope for peace.

I said to her, "If only we could be as peaceful as this lake appears today."

"Ah," she said. "Yes. But underneath that peaceful and placid water is a volcano. Human beings are here to learn, not just to be happy, but to learn."

"It's quite upsetting when you really think about it," I said. "How can we produce a peaceful society when we are all so different?"

She looked at me and said, "Yes, Guatemala is very much like what you're saying. There's always an upset, whether it's with the government or politics or one village that decides they want to fight another village for some reason or another, and it is not a happy thing. I wish there was something that we could do about this, but it doesn't seem to be in the cards. What did you come here to learn?" she asked me.

"Well, I came into this life to learn about sacred work, about teaching, about taking my power as a woman, understanding how my creativity is a huge asset of my power. Does that seem familiar?" I asked.

"Oh, yes," she said, running her hands over the vertical threads. "Take these threads. Today many of our people don't weave like I do. I use this backstrap loom because it's ancient. It gives me a feeling of our people as they have always been. We have a culture. We are so fortunate to have this particular way of life. It's very old, and we as shamans help with all of this very, very much."

I sat back on my heels and wondered about all of the things that she had just said. "How extraordinary human life can be," I said. "And how we ruin it."

"Well," she said, "yes, we so often ruin it. But we also learn great things, and it is the learning that is the important thing."

"Life is magical, which is like the word 'magician' in many languages," I said.

"Yes, it is true. And it is also true that if I were to call you a 'magician' in my village, the people would be terrified of you because they would think you are a black magician."

I said, "Oh, no. That's not for me!"

She said, "Well, that's a good thing! Thought is like throwing a pebble into the water. It ripples and touches so many."

The air was pure and clear. It made me feel good. I told Painted Bird, "I just feel so good, so happy here. It's beautiful. I wish I could be here alot."

She smiled. "Well, you can, you know. You are always welcome. There is much that we can teach you. But first let's talk about the warp and the weft of a weaving. The warp threads are the vertical threads we have been talking about. They are the anchoring threads that hold the weaving together."

"The pragmatic threads," I offered.

Painted Bird thought for a moment. Then she said, "When you say 'pragmatic,' you speak of enlightenment. The warp threads are the strong pragmatic threads that represent how well you hold power within your own being. Symbolically, they are the warp threads of your dreams, the anchoring threads of your existence. Do you understand?" She looked up at me with such serenity.

"Yes, I do," I smiled. This is something that Agnes and I had spoken of so often, using different terms and analogies but talking about the same thing, the framework with which we anchor ourselves in life before moving into any act of power. For me, that anchor is my Oneness with the Great Spirit and all of life, which leads me to my own personal truth. That is how I build and hold true power, through divine Oneness.

Painted Bird continued, "The warp threads are picked from the places of origin, the places of power of Mother Earth. They come from the water powers, the water babies that turn an unfathomable existence in the darkness, waiting to be born into the light through the ability of your sacred fingers and your sacred thought. They are given birth through the anchoring of the physical world and spirit, creating the framework to weave divine inspiration into an actual form."

She paused for a moment and then started weaving a horizontal thread through the vertical threads on her loom.

"I'm talking about the beauty, now," she continued. "I'm moving into the beauty that crosses over the vertical lines of strength. These are the weft threads of the weaving, the horizontal threads that weave patterns through the anchoring threads. Artists oftentimes forget their vertical lines, the anchoring lines of their lives. They want only to focus on the beauty that crosses over and between these threads. However, the vertical quality is incredibly important. They need to have a firm foundation in the physical world in order to make a living.

"The directional cross is always there, your foundation and how you weave through it the patterns of beauty and magic in your life. There is so much magic in the warp and the weft of a weaving and the way they are placed on the loom. I try to represent that magic with color. Color has a true voice of its own. Color has a very special quality which each person feels differently."

"I've never really thought about color that way," I said.

"Well," she said, "why don't you pick the colors that you would like to see? You pick the colors that are here for you. You will find it exciting as we put them together. I think I will make this *huipile* for you. I think that would help you and bring you joy."

I picked out yellow, orange, red, turquoise blue and a lovely kind of wheat-like yarn. They were beautiful.

I said, "Well, these are all my colors."

She said, "Yes, I know." She put red together with turquoise, and the purple behind it, where it added so much depth. And she said, "That purple represents the depth of your soul. It is as deep as that lake, and you cannot reach the bottom. And that's you."

"Thank you for seeing me," I said, quietly.

"The color that you bring through the fibers going across the weaving horizontally, the weft threads of the weaving, the threads that give it texture and patterns. The weft threads of your dreams are what give your life texture. They are the essential elements that fill your life with meaning, the subtle threads of perception and awareness that represent your own perspective of reality, the subtleties and the perception of the beauty of your life as an art form. Never forget them," she said. "They are what bring the sacred cross into your weaving and into your life."

"I won't," I said. "I won't ever forget such a beautiful teaching. Thank you."

"Go up and get some tortillas and cheese," she said. "You must be starving."

"I am. Thank you so much. I love you." I gave her a big hug.

Circling Back: "Living a Life of Magic"

Magic, what a wonderful part of life!

Magic is what fills our souls with joy, the hope that is found in each new sunrise. It is what warms our bones on a cold winter day as the sun glints off the frozen snow, creating miniature prisms of dancing light that capture our imagination and catapult us into a very special place. It is what cools us down when it is 112° in the shade and we feel the caress of a gentle breeze on our cheek. Magic is the love that we experience when we see a newborn child or look into the wisdom that is reflected in the eyes of the oldest person we've ever met.

Like the power of Stonehenge, magic is part of the unknowable, that which we cannot describe but which exists and makes our lives extraordinary. It is part of the goodness of our spirit, the mysterious and intriguing aspect that makes our spiritual life so relevant no matter what, the colors and designs of the warp and weft threads of our lives.

Magic is part of the fantastic and the fantastical experience of life, and we do need both. This world of ours is filled with so much that is truly wonderful and miraculous. It is also filled with much that is chaotic, stressful and destructive. On any given day, you and I experience more bedlam than the world has ever known simply because we chose to be born into this world at this important juncture in human history. This is not something that Mother Earth or some alien beings from another planet did to us. It is what we humans have done to ourselves, and I believe that each of us knows, deep within our own being, in the middle of the bedlam, that we are equally capable of doing something about it.

Such is the power of magic, that it can transform even the darkest of times into the promise of a new and better world if only we will focus on the genius of human ingenuity and the brilliance of the natural world, instead of focusing on the distractions.

Magic also has its 'other side,' the side of magic that we refer to as 'magic thinking' where, like Cinderella, you find yourself waiting for some singular person or event to come along and magically make everything in your life better so that you can somehow live happily ever after. We all need these flights of fantasy once in a while, but you know you are in trouble when you find yourself waiting . . . and waiting . . . and waiting, until you wake up one day and life isn't magical anymore because you've wasted it on magic thinking instead of acting on your dreams.

To have power in life, you must take power; it is never just given to you. When you are engaged in magic thinking, you bleed off your heat and you bleed off your power, no matter how long you wait or how ardently you wish, because magic thinking is not real.

Magic, however, is as real as anything you will ever see, touch, feel, taste or hear. Magic is understanding where God is in your life, understanding that there is a way to hold an impeccability that is completely comprehensible and reasonable. It is accepting that there is more to life than what you see.

Magic is what happens when something comes out of the unknown, an epiphany of understanding, and suddenly you can see the entirety of a difficult and perplexing dilemma, where it started, where it went wrong, perhaps, and what to do about it.

Do you remember the Michael Crighton film *Fear*, where there were monsters in the world and the people couldn't figure out where the monsters were coming from? They thought they were being attacked by some kind of evil, supernatural force -- until all of a sudden they realized that the monsters were coming out of them because of the way they were thinking. It wasn't that they wanted the monsters; they just wanted to bleed off the energy that was taking them towards enlightenment because enlightenment was something they had never experienced before and it frightened them.

Why does this happen? It happens because we are conditioned beings who are afraid of the very perfection that we are simply because we've never been allowed or allowed ourselves to experience it. That is why we create Cinderella and Peter Pan fantasies in our lives, to give us a sense of power and perfection that we are afraid we, ourselves, don't really have. We become conditioned away from our own power at a very young age. That conditioning separates us from the passion and intensity of living our own truth in the world. We become separated from the brilliant vibrancy of our inner life which so animates us in childhood, making us invincible!

This inner life, where you are one with the Great Spirit, is your spiritual life force. Inspiration comes from your spiritual life force: inspiration, the fuel that is needed in all of your actions in life. When you are separated from inspiration, your own acts of power are going to be very weak, if they exist at all.

How can you connect with your spiritual life force, with inspiration and all of the passion and intensity of living your own truth in the world? How can you transform your life into a life of magic?

Begin by acknowledging that what we usually call 'coincidence,' like someone calling and you know who it is before the phone rings, is really a part of the magic of life. Acknowledge and accept it as a gift of consciousness from the universe.

Magic is a consciousness, a joyous attitude toward living. Make a conscious choice to shift out of negative states of perception, even if you have to fake it. When you find yourself falling into the 'blues,' learn something new. Ask yourself, "Who would want to be near me when I am feeling so miserable?" Then shift your attitude by getting up and moving. Change positions as you change your mindset to a state of conscious choice. Run, exercise, do research on your favorite subject and experience the joy of learning something new.

Shift your emotional state. See yourself as a spirit with a physical body, rather than a body with a possible spirit, and let spiritual life force be your guiding strength in life. Your spiritual life force is what makes the difference between living a life of magic and living a life of magic thinking. And it is the one thing in this entire world over which you have the most control! Find your spiritual life force now, and live the glorious life of magic that is waiting for you.

4

RUBY PLENTY CHIEFS

I FEEL THAT IT'S IMPORTANT to speak of Ruby Plenty Chiefs, who has been one of the very great teachers of my life. She is sometimes a terrifying woman, endearing and terrifying at the same time. She is terrifying in her tantrums. She is terrifying in her teaching techniques and her demands, yet kind, with a heart of pure gold in her healing process. Always, her eyes shine like polished abalone shells.

She can also be a fearsome sight. As a young girl, she was raped by surveyors who came into her cabin, cruelly violated her and then blinded her with the points of their compasses so that she could never identify them. She was supposed to be married soon after, which, of course, became socially taboo after the rape, and she just wanted to die.

She was only about 16 years old at the time, and she lived with her father. He was an extraordinary man for his time. He was sensitive. He understood his young daughter. He did not blame her or make her feel that she was bad in some way, like many of the other people did. Instead, he found a Soto medicine man to help her.

Ruby didn't want to go to see this medicine man. She didn't want to live. But her father bundled her up and took her to an obscure cabin and an obscure medicine man about whom most people knew nothing. Her father knew this man and knew that he would know how to heal his daughter, and he left her with complete trust in a very, very old man in a little hut in the woods.

An elder woman would come in to care for the old man, bringing him food and keeping him healthy and strong through the long winters.

Ruby was with him for a long time, while he fed her deer meat. The deer is a very sacred animal to Native American cultures, sacred because it is the animal of the sacred give-away. It gives its own life so that others may live. Native spirituality teaches that whatever you take from the universe, you must give back in like kind. This means that you never take for foolish reasons. You never kill for sport. You never steal for the sake of gaining riches. When the hunter prepares for the hunt, a great ceremony and honoring of the animals to be hunted takes place. After the hunt, every morsel of the fallen animal is used. Nothing is left to waste. Wastefulness is a dishonoring of the great and abundant spirit of Mother Earth and all of her creatures. This is how Native peoples give back to the universe what they take for their survival, by treating everything with sacredness, by honoring its spirit and its flesh as they would honor their own.

It was this give-away that this elder shaman man had realized many years ago. Somehow he had discovered that through the give-away of the deer, those who ate its meat could regain their vision. His work was to restore vision to this beautiful young girl. He also worked with her heart, a heart that had been so broken that it, too, was ill.

Many things in Ruby's body were beginning to malfunction, like her liver. As this medicine healer slowly fed her only deer meat, he began also to work with her in the dreamtime, showing her how to see places of magic that are so abundant on other levels of awareness. He helped her to realize that even if you lose an arm, the electromagnetic field that was your arm, the astral field of your arm is perhaps a better way to say it, the astral form of your arm is still there. You can learn to feel and sense and 'see' with this astral form. Somehow, eating deer meat facilitates this remarkable way of perception.

In a sense, he helped give Ruby back her eyes. Through him, she discovered the astral form of her eyes. At one point, he even put prosthetic eyeballs into her eye sockets. She learned to blink her eyes once again, to feel that maybe she was still as beautiful as she had always been. He made a special viscous-like ointment out of herbs to put in her eyes, which made them stop hurting her so. In all of the years that I have known Ruby, her eyes have never hurt her.

But the most interesting thing about what he had done with her eyes is that when light shines from the sun or the moon, her eyes look like mirrors, truly like mirrors. They reflect, and it is an arresting thing to see that in a woman's face. It is shocking and, if she were so inclined, she could frighten you terribly. It wouldn't be hard to do.

This medicine healer worked with her throughout an entire winter, and then through another set of seasons. One day Ruby's father came to see her, and as she told me about him I realized that my soul will be moved throughout eternity by the love that she told me she felt in her father's presence. She still had another season to go in this hut in the woods. She had not yet learned how to truly 'see' as she does now, but she was beginning to regain her confidence. She had learned how to move around the cabin, how to gather water, how to walk down a trail and feel the wind on her skin and in her hair without being frightened. And she had begun to reawaken with the great, unconditional love of Divine spirit.

She also learned many things about sensibilities from this old man so that now, if you are around Ruby, there is no way in the world that you can fool her. She senses a lie. She feels it. She knows it's there. She knows people better than you and I ever could. And she eats deer meat. The deer meat somehow helps her to find vision through her skin. That's what the old man told me, "She sees through her skin."

And she does. She doesn't often see details, although once in awhile she will see a color that I have missed. But she can actually see the colors that you wear. She 'sees' color, senses the vibration and energy of color. It is astonishing. I don't know how to explain it. It is a miracle.

Of course it's a miracle, but then again, it's a miracle that we are all alive. How do we see through our eyes? I don't know the physiology of being sighted, but the vision is there and it is a gift. Ruby began to realize the gift that sight is, this gift that we take so for granted, and she became initiated into a whole other world of visioning. I hope you can feel what it is I am trying to say. Words can be so inadequate, but Ruby often sees things in the physical world that sighted people completely miss.

Ruby also sees through the bottoms of her feet. There are times when I will find her sitting in a chair with her feet up, and her bare feet will somehow be giving her the sight of the sunset. We have sat together and talked about the panoramic splendor of a given sunset on many occasions.

The vision of the sunset that her bare feet give her brings her such joy. That joy fills her with love, love for me, love for her friends. Her love for the women of the Sisterhood of the Shields is very deep and profound. It actually encompasses the rebuilding of cellular structure in those about whom she cares. She sees them in their own states of perfection, sees them as god or goddess beings and somehow has the ability to bring their cellular body into that aspect of her dreaming.

I, too, have experienced this as a healer, where I will look at people and see their perfection and their beauty. This has often tricked me, because people don't necessarily live in the space of their beauty. They sometimes live in a whole other area of consciousness, one which may be thoroughly corrupted. And I can have trouble seeing that corruption; it is so foreign to my experience of life. I see only the potential of their beauty. It takes both Ruby and Agnes to help me with that

I used to say to Ruby, "You know, we could use some funding here to build some buildings for our school, a museum, a place where people could come, a campus, to work and study with all of you." A horrified look would cross all of their faces.

"Oh," Ruby would say, emphatically. "No, no, no. That is not our purpose in this life. Our purpose is to heal this earth and heal people on the other side of the veil, bringing wisdom and knowledge back to the people in the relative world. No, no, no," she would say.

I would counter, "But Ruby, you have an undeniable ability to see things. Maybe we should take you to Las Vegas and do some gambling."

Well, the Sisterhood thought this was the funniest thing in the whole wide world. One time, they brought out a collection of wooden coin-like objects, which were actually pieces of a game, similar to Apache dominos, that you could use for divining, for healing. They all said, "These are the only gambling pieces we will ever use." So, that was the end of that discussion. Ruby has never used her abilities for anything other than what she has been trained to be, a healer.

Needless to say, Ruby is a different kind of person whose life experience is vastly different from anything any of us has ever had. When she works with me, she has chosen to be very tough on me. Oftentimes, she has made things enormously difficult for me.

On the occasion of our very first meeting, she scared me out of my wits by making me skin a deer as night fell in the high mountains. That almost put me into a coma. It was late in the day in a vast and imposing wilderness where I had never been before. There was no escape, and this total stranger was tossing around deer knives like they were toothpicks, demanding that I skin a deer or leave.

Years have passed since then, but when we work together, Ruby has the most exquisite way of going right to the one place that I am most vulnerable. That very first night, she knew that I was carrying very deep-seated fears; she knew that I would never be able to receive the wisdom that the Sisterhood had to impart to me as long as I lived in those fears. Skinning that deer was, for me, the first and ultimate test, especially since there was no true danger associated with it. If I had been unable to overcome my fear and allow her to teach me how to skin a deer, how could I ever become willing to transcend the bounds of my other self-imposed limitations?

Even today, no matter how hard I try to be strong and gild my qualms over with gold so that Ruby will love me, she always finds that little place where I am hiding from my vulnerability. Then she crawls right in there and pays it a whole lot of attention until it hurts so hard that I can't ignore it. I become afraid, but I grow from it. And Ruby knows it. That is her way of teaching me. At the same time, I would be very concerned to have anyone I didn't know well work with her, because she is very tough.

She feels pointedly that if you can't take it, then you shouldn't be there in the first place. Of course, we don't always know what we are getting ourselves into, until we get there. Because of her strength, however, Ruby has taken me way beyond the point where I was convinced I would fall apart, many times. She has given me an endurance that I didn't have before I met her. I am strong, very strong, but I needed to be stronger and she brought me there.

Many people have said that they would have trouble with the way Ruby treats me, as did I for all of my early work with these women. Today, however, I see it as Ruby play-acting, being a naughty child or a pugnacious, picky old lady, to get my attention. When she acts like that, I know she has seen something in me that I need to address, that I am hiding from myself.

Each of the women of the Sisterhood has her own way of speaking, of working, of healing. I suspect that they take on these other personas mostly when I am around. They play until I get so frustrated with the awful seriousness with which I have taken myself that I just give up and start playing, too. It is only then that true vision can enter. Then we all play together; we all act like that. You must understand that my meetings with these women of high degree are a process of learning and always will be. Today, we learn from each other and we teach each other.

We teach each other on many different harmonic levels of consciousness. My experience of this is that Agnes brings in what I experience as a 'soprano' element. Ruby will bring in percussion and Twin Dreamers will bring in the violin, and it all goes together. Then I start playing a flute, all within our sensory imaginations, and something is created, an orchestra of words, a harmony, a new harmony of actions that heals us all in some way.

I have written of my life with these women as I have experienced it. And when you read my words, if you will set aside doubt and criticism, and assume, instead, that I wouldn't bother dedicating my life to some kind of silly nonsense, if you will move along with me and listen, letting your heart and soul go into the words, all of a sudden, you, also, will be transported. Then you will see that all of the difficulty is really a gift, a harmony written with the sacred sounds of the Sisterhood that takes you to the very place you most want to go.

The circle of shaman medicine people in our world is a true gift to us all. They are exceptional people from only a few places on earth who bring all-encompassing gifts to the world. They are highly trained and have devoted their entire lives to higher learning. Ruby is one of this circle.

Circling Back: "The Law of Grace"

Hardship happens to everyone, and it can be our greatest teacher in life. Through the struggle to overcome adversity, you awaken strength and courage within you that you might otherwise have completely missed. To me, Ruby's life story brings this home with profound clarity. It is true, as the Roman philosopher Horace wrote, *"Adversity reveals genius, prosperity conceals it."* (Quintus Horatius Flaccus, 65 BC-8 BC.)

When we go through difficult times, it is easy to fall into the trap of fighting with life. We think that if we fight against what is happening, we are actually doing something favorable. We brace ourselves for battle. We adopt a grim determination, become rigid, thinking that somehow inflexibility makes us stronger.

What we don't realize is that when we do this, we are actually turning our world into a battleground where the battle is against our own selves. Worse, we are inviting in the darkness and negativity of the battleground. The way you approach any situation you face in life can actually determine the success or failure of your mission. When you engage negativity in battle, you give it energy. You give it yourself as the target. Negativity has a huge mouth, one that will devour you if you allow it, for what it wants more than anything else is to be fed. By becoming grim, you cut yourself off from the light. By becoming rigid, you give up the ability to bend and sway, to move with the storm like a willow in the wind. It is precisely its flexibility that allows the willow to survive.

We forget that there is a difference between doing battle and being strong.

There is no question but that there is darkness in the world, not in the form of evil spirits lurking about, waiting to catch you unawares, which is usually silliness, but rather in our own daily ignorance of harmonious living and how that actually happens.

It is a spiritual axiom that when darkness comes, you must honor it for the lessons it has come to teach you. This darkness can be a great messenger, for it always comes for a reason. Light a candle to the adversity that carries darkness on its back and bring in the light. Ask the adversity what it has come to teach you, and then turn towards the light. If you stare at darkness for too long, it will begin to stare back. It will begin to entice you as it studies your rhythms and plays upon your frailties, especially your fractured emotions and the roof chatter that sets in.

Don't let your mind or your emotions engage you in battle. That is when you lose before you even get started. If you can look at adversity as an opportunity to learn and to grow, you will find within it teachings of clarity, strength and wisdom that you can find, perhaps, nowhere else in life.

19th century Harvard law professor and psychologist William James framed it so clearly when he wrote, "There is a law in psychology that if you form a picture in your mind of what you would like to be, and you keep and hold that picture there long enough, you will become exactly as you have been thinking." Can you see the immediate trap in engaging life as a battleground against the difficulties of your life? You may think that by fighting, you are building strength. What you are really doing is creating a person you don't want to become. If you hold the picture of fighting and negativity in your mind long enough, you will become it.

In the shaman's world view, you don't fight against anything. When difficulties arise, as they will, become the solution, not the victim forever bemoaning your fate. Actually imagine what it feels like to be in the solution instead of the problem. Then allow that feeling to empower you until you become it.

As you imagine yourself in the solution, your heart begins to expand and you become grateful for all of the things that are actually right in your life. When you bring these to the forefront of your consciousness, they become your cushion and your foundation. You strengthen that foundation by being grateful for it.

Gratitude energizes you. It is a state of being which is filled with strength, wisdom, endurance and all the courage you need to move through hardship in an enlightened, intended way. Gratitude brings you into the present moment, which is where your strength and your power are always found.

Become conscious and fully present in the moment. When you are fully present in the moment, you discover a quality of being alert which I understand as coming from your very life force. This alertness is not something you can understand with your ego mind, which would probably be desperately engaged in what it believes to be a life-and-death-struggle with your problem, anyway. Instead, use the brilliance of your analytical mind to help you chart your path forward. The ego is incapable of finding its way to the present moment; it has other things which it considers far more important. The problem, of course, is that full awareness is always in the present moment.

If you follow the energy and vision of being present and alert in the moment, you will naturally move into your own life force. This is when you remember that you are One with the Great Sprit and everything in life. God is not some entity which is outside of you. God is within you and part of you, just as you are part of and within God. There is no greater power in the world than life force, which is God.

When you allow yourself to become one with the Great Spirit, you transcend the dimensions of ordinary life. You move into your higher consciousness, where your vision is truly unlimited, unclouded by the distractions of judgment, fear, jealousy and anger. Now you can actually begin to see what it is you can do to change the circumstances of your hardship and create a positive solution.

Try this the next time you feel weighted down by problems. The next time hardship moves into your hut and it feels like the roof is going to cave in, sit in silence and allow your mind to empty of all its distractions. This may be difficult in the beginning, because our minds are constantly at work, chattering at us about everything and nothing. Researchers have determined that the average person is capable of reading comfortably at about 250-300 words per minute and speed-reading at up to 800 w.p.m. with training. We listen comfortably at about 200-300 words per minute, which is fairly close to the speed at which we speak.

Our thoughts, on the other hand, go at warp speed. Their speed is impossible to quantify because there are so many different parts of the brain involved at the same time, each generating its own brain waves at its own individual speed. While you are reading a book, one part of your brain is working with your eyes to read and translate the letters into words, while other parts are interpreting the material for you, while still other parts of your brain are engaged in thoughts that have nothing to do with what you are reading.

So quieting the mind, emptying it of all distractions, can be difficult in the beginning. But millions of people the world over who have learned to meditate and practice yoga are here to tell you that it can be done! What I urge you to do is to practice sha-man breathing, which is focusing on your breathing as you inhale the breath of the Great Spirit deeply into your belly. Consciously cycle it through the blood and cells of your body, and then exhale sharply. As you exhale, see all thoughts and distractions leave with your breath.

Do this three or four times, and then begin to breathe deeply and rhythmically. Follow each breath in and out with your mind. Distractions will flit through, but don't hook onto them. Let them go. Remember that they can only capture your attention if you give it to them, so don't give it to them. Simply let them float through you as you stay focused on your breathing.

Begin to envision yourself moving toward a state of grace. Don't try to define that grace or what it should 'feel' like or 'look' like. This is a distraction. Just envision yourself moving toward a 'state of grace' as you focus on your breathing.

Sit in silence and empty yourself of distractions, coming fully into the present moment. You will begin to find the alertness of being fully in the moment.

Now bring in your intent and set it to follow this alertness to your higher consciousness and the heart of your very life force. Feel your heart beating with the heart of the Great Spirit. Feel your heart beating with the rhythms of life force as it moves through the universe and across our great Mother Earth. You don't have to do anything to move into this life force, because it is already within you. Just allow yourself to experience it, perhaps for the very first time.

Your awareness of the life force within you will move you into gratitude. You may have to coax yourself to find gratitude. If the mind starts throwing other 'real emergencies' at you, simply go back to your breathing and reconnect with your life force in a conscious and intended way. Then follow that life force back to

Oneness with the Great Spirit and gratitude for all that is right and good in your life.

Gratitude is a state of being that will guide you into a positive, constructive state of doing with more clarity than you may, at first, believe possible.

Gratitude is our way of saying, "Thank you," to the Great Spirit for all of the gifts of life which surround us always, even when we don't feel them. When you are in gratitude, you are in the celebration of thankfulness, which is a great and an energizing force.

This is the law of grace: surviving hardship through gratitude.

It is the darkness which defines the light. If you choose to move into the darkness, you will cut yourself off from the light. If you choose to move into the light, you begin to see the darkness for the illusion that it is as you follow the light into gratitude.

Then astonishing things begin to happen to the hardships of your life: the solutions you seek will come to you. You may not understand them at first. They may not be what you thought you wanted or expected them to be. That's alright. They are there for you. You find them through connecting with the God force within you. Once you are connected with that God force, get up and move around. Infuse yourself with it through movement. Go for a walk and discover yourself walking in unison with your surroundings in a conscious way. Begin to look at the world around you through eyes of gratitude and move through it with grace. The solutions you seek will show themselves to you. It will happen.

5

AMY HUMMINGBIRD WING I
The Melipona

AMY HUMMINGBIRD WING is the Wanderer. Like a hummingbird, she wanders from one place to another. She migrates from the north to the south for thousands of miles.

She is a warrior. When Sin Corazón was thrown out of the Sisterhood of the Shields for stealing the Shaman's Jewel, the darkness of sorcery was trying to wage a huge war against the light. Amy Hummingbird Wing was very powerful and prominent in not letting that happen.

Amy is a native woman from South America. She is very elder. She has survived the ruination of her country from rebels, power shifts, and the hatred visited upon indigenous peoples by the ruling class and the government. She has survived it all.

One of the ways she has been able to remain the magnificent woman she is in her essence is by wandering. She wanders from town to town in an old, two-tone green truck which she has driven all over South America, the Yucatán and Central America. When she arrives at a new town, she hides her truck in the underbrush in the most incredible ways. Then she wanders into the area and gets to know the people. She becomes like the hummingbird, taking the sweet nectar of wisdom that the people of one village give her and sharing it with the people of the next village. She is a collector of honey.

Amy Hummingbird Wing is a woman of power, "one who knows how," a shaman woman. She is a healer in the dimensions of spirit as she wanders the dimensions of the physical, collecting honey and dispensing it wherever she goes.

When I was in the south of Mexico with Zoila a very long time ago, Amy gave me a beautiful teaching. I had been walking through the jungle with Zoila, working on things that she had taught me, when she unexpectedly disappeared into the agave and underbrush. Out of nowhere, coming toward me on the trail, was an elder woman who looked very familiar.

As I came up to her, I said, "I know you. I *see* you."

She laughed and touched my forehead with her thumb. She was dressed in a pink and yellow *huipile* and a woven skirt in blue with embroidered stitching along the hem. She wore worn leather sandals and many silver necklaces from Guatemala, South America, and the Yucatán. Her earrings were long and beautiful, hanging all the way down to her shoulders. She had on a hat that must have been at least a hundred years old. It was made of straw in an odd weave and tilted jauntily on her head, giving her a look of power and, somehow, humor.

She said in broken English, "Little Wolf! I have not seen you in a long time, but I have seen you in the dreaming circles."

When we cannot be together, the women of the Sisterhood of the Shields know how to travel the dimensions of the ethers and other planes of existence and join together in the sacred dreamtime.

"Yes. It is so wonderful to meet you here," I exclaimed, delighted. "Why are you here?"

"To see you," she replied.

I started to sputter. I couldn't imagine how she had gotten there, where she had come from, or why Zoila hadn't mentioned it.

"Come. I have something to show you," she said, as she dug in her woven cotton bag. It had large roses embroidered on it and looked as if it had come from Guatemala, from Solala, perhaps. She took out of its depths some netting that she put over her head. Then she put a netting over me that went all the way to the ground.

"Just hold the edges with your fingers," she said. "I want to take you somewhere, and you need the netting."

We walked carefully through the underbrush filled with agave and a few higher trees that glistened in the sunshine, after the morning's early rain. We came to a hut in the clearing.

"I didn't know this hut was here," I said in surprise. "Whose is it?"

Amy just looked at me and said, "Come. Pay attention."

I followed her. We came to beehives that were set behind the hut. Bees were flying in and out all over the place.

"Keep your netting on. I don't think you will need it, but you might."

I didn't particularly want to get stung by a bee, but I followed her as she walked over to one of the beehives, holding tight to the netting. She put on a pair of gloves and then took the top off the beehive as bees swarmed everywhere and all over her. I stood back and watched as she took out a honeycomb. She did some things with her fingers and collected some honey into a little jar that was sitting there. Suddenly all the bees flew away and left her alone. She was singing under her breath, very softly in *Quiché,* a Mayan language native to Guatemala, as she did a ceremony around the beehive, circling it four times sunwise. Then she offered the honey to Sky Father and Earth Mother, and to the elementals.

She turned to me and said, "Come. We are going to do ceremony together.

We walked down a trail near the beehives, going deeper into a grove of *Chak Kuyché* trees until we came to a little hut with a thatched roof of the trees, like a *palapa* or Tiki hut that you would find on the beach. As we approached, I noticed that there was a pile of old logs tied into the shape of a pyramid. I was surprised when Amy turned around and took the netting off of me, folding it neatly and putting it, along with her own folded netting, into one of the bags she was carrying. She set the bags down as we sat on the ground near the *palapa,* and she spoke to me about her bees.

"The African bees that we have just seen and some European bees are faster producers than *melipona* bees," she said. "The *melipona* is the ancient bee of the Yucatán and the Mayan people, and it holds a very special place in our lives. But the other bees produce much faster. Sometimes, if there is a full moon, they will work all night long gathering nectar, while the *melipona* bee tends to awaken midday and is very selective about which flowers it picks from. It is an incredible thing to watch *the melipona* bees and we will see them very soon."

We sat near the *palapa* and I watched the sunlight around us coming through the trees, splashes of light that looked like *kachinas* dancing across the clearing. Suddenly, a bee came directly towards me, and then many more, and I started to dodge them and waive my hands stupidly in the air.

Amy put her hand on my shoulder and said, "Lynn. Lynn, relax. These bees are stingless bees and they are very different from the bees you are used to."

She reached out her hand and a bee lit on the back of it. I stared in disbelief and couldn't believe what I was seeing. The bee was tiny like a small insect, like a fly with great big eyes.

I laughed and said, "Their eyes are almost like the big eyes of a Chihuahua dog, they don't really fit their tiny bodies."

She laughed and said, "They are very precious. In ancient times, these bees were our sustenance and our trade beads. Their honey is white and has almost a citrus taste, and it has many medicinal qualities. It heals all kinds of things. This honey was traded from one village to another like your people use money. Today we still trade the honey for medicinal purposes. It is a very different honey from any you have ever had before. Come. Let's look in one of those logs."

I followed her tentatively because I couldn't believe there was a non-stinging bee. As we walked to the pyramid of logs, Amy reached up to one of the *Kuyché* trees, pulled a few leaves off and rubbed them between her hands. Then she rubbed them on her forehead and her cheeks. She indicated that I should do the same, and I did. With song, a chanting, she moved in a circle around the pyramid of logs singing in her *Quiché* language, she was praying, lifting her arms as if to a God, and praying some more.

When she was finished, she came over to me and said, "There are *melapona* beehives in these logs. I am praying and I would like you to do that, also. Pray to the God that loves and protects the *melipona*. Often we serve a wine when we do this ceremony, but today I chose not to do that. I would like you to offer a prayer in silence, if you will, and then I would like the Green One to hear your voice. I want you to ask for the purification of your soul and the purification of the world towards all living things."

She began moving around the *palapa* and the pyramid of logs again and I noticed for the first time, as she lit them, that there were thirteen candles ringing us.

When she finished lighting the candles, she said to me, "Thirteen is a very sacred number with the Mayan, as you know. It is a number that is used particularly in association with the keepers of the stingless bees. It is part of our tradition and part of our honoring. We pray to *Ah-Muzen-Cab*, a Mayan bee god. At the site of Tulum, you can see imprints of him. We have always prayed to him for safety and long life and survival. He is also known a Descending God. When you go to the beehives or see the stingless bees playing somewhere, always pray to *Ah-Muzen-Cab* and thank him for helping these bees survive."

She then explained to me that the *melipona* bees had almost become extinct. "They were almost gone from us at one point, but they are coming back now and it is very important that we honor both the *melipona* and *Ah-Mutzen-Cab.*"

As I looked at the pyramid of old logs with new eyes, I said to Amy, "Isn't it interesting that in this time when the great trees are falling, these bees have hidden their hives in the fallen trees and are now starting to become back into the world. There is something about that which is very special, sacred, as you have said."

After we completed our ceremony, she said to me, "Now it is time to talk to you about a wanderer," and she led me back the way we had come, until we reached the small hut. When we entered, it was obvious that she had been there for a few days. The bed was beautifully made, covered by a blanket of woven cotton. There was a place for a fire. There were a few utensils for cooking. There was a dirt floor. Where we sat, shelves of beautiful abalone shells glinted in the sunlight coming through the cracks in the hut, which was made of adobe and reeds.

She drew a wavy line in the dirt of the floor and said, "Does this mean anything to you?"

"Well, it could be a snake," I offered.

"This is the trail of the wanderer," she said.

"Is it a definite trail?"

"No. Spirit pulls me from village to village. I have had family. I have taken seeds from all over this part of the world, seeds that I collect in seed pots for later generations." She pointed to the side of the hut that was in shadows, and I saw small, rounded pots which she had made. She walked over and picked one up, bringing it to me.

She sat down next to me and said, "Here. You hold this, the seeds of wisdom, the seeds of future plants that will feed our people. Seeds are precious. They are everything. The seeds are sacred and bring you holy goodness."

She made several signs with her hands. "Have you ever wondered about my name? What is my name?" she asked in very broken English.

"Amy Hummingbird Wing."

"Yes. What does the hummingbird do?"

"It flies with great strength and power. Some migrate thousands of miles, from north to south and back to the north."

"Yes," she responded. "That is my way. What is the importance of that?"

"I don't know," I answered. "You are a warrior. That I know. And you help anyone who is in a fight with themselves or with someone else."

"What I do is collect honey. I collect the sweetness of life. I collect the honey and I bring it to people. It gives them immunity from disease. This," she said, holding up the jar of honey she had just collected, "is very special honey, but honey nevertheless. The bees all know me. I am one of them.

"They know that I flutter," she continued, wiggling her shoulders. "They know that I take only so much honey. Bears love me. Remember Betty Fast Bear? She loves me. She is a great teacher of hibernation, of dreaming. We know each other quite well. She shares in my honey. She gathers honey, as well, but the bees don't like her nearly as well as they like me, because I'm more careful. I am like the hummingbird. I take this honey, this wisdom, from

65

village to village. I take the seeds, too, and help the people plant them. I feed their bodies in many, many ways. And I teach them wisdom and the strength of spirit."

Amy began to laugh. Taking a few seeds from the shelf, she poured them into one of the seed pots. Her toothless laughter was contagious. Then she put her arms around me and rocked us both, back and forth, as she gave me some honey.

"See. This will make you strong and fill you with joy and love."

It was so sweet, this honey, and darker in color than I was used to. We shared the honey until it was all gone.

Then Amy said to me, "It is time for us to part now, my friend."

I so didn't want this day to end. There was so much I wanted to learn and experience with this remarkable woman. It was with true reluctance that I started back down the path to Zoila's house, not knowing whether I would ever have the opportunity to be with Amy again.

When I arrived back at Zoila's, she and her family were preparing for a celebration in the village. They tried to teach me how to make good tortillas. It was hopeless, but we laughed, covered with flour, and much later, we went to sleep.

Circling Back: "Through the Eyes of a Spiritual Warrior"

Mother Earth is the greatest schoolhouse we will ever have in this life, if we would but learn to listen to her.

I am always fascinated by the ancient Mayans, who observed and charted the movement of the planets and stars through the heavens and the winds and waters across the land more than any other civilization on earth, drawing knowledge and wisdom from the ways in which all things interact.

When you study the few Mayan codices that survived the *conquistadorés*, or work with contemporary Mayan healers like Zoila or Jaguar Woman, you discover how thoroughly these ancient people understood that the natural world is our first teacher and ultimate task-master. They used the knowledge and wisdom that Mother Earth and Father Sky taught them to chart their course through life. Because they understood the movement of the planets and the stars, the solar winds and energy throughout the universe, they were able to predict with remarkable accuracy the events not only of their own times but also earth changes for hundreds of years into the future, including the configuration of heavenly bodies that will occur in our own time in the year 2012.

I have had the opportunity to witness firsthand how well the Mayans understood both the energies of nature and the nature of human beings in ways that our modern psychology is only beginning to glean, and to participate in some of the elaborate initiations they created to teach their young how to live in harmony with their world. I have learned first-hand what a remarkable way this is to experience life!

The word "shaman" is actually Tungusic in origin, from the indigenous Tungusic peoples of Siberia who conceive of the universe as a living organism: *šamán,* "one who knows," one who is able to divine the hidden and use the powers of the spirit world to heal.

Although they are called differently and work in somewhat different fashion across the world, the *šamán*—those who know and enter the spirit world at will, who go into the great mystery of the unseen to bring back the power and magic of healing wisdom to the physical world, the shamans—have been a vital part of the fabric of humanity in every corner of this earth for tens of thousands of years, continuing to the present day. Because it is practiced differently and known by different names in different cultures, however, there is no singular expression either for the *šamán* or for what these healers do. Modern English has come up with the term "shamanism" to embrace this world, without offense to any of the many magnificent differences in the way that the sacred medicine of spirit is known, understood and practiced around the globe.

The shamanism of the Sisterhood of the Shields is a shamanism based on the principles of the sacred feminine that are over ten thousand years old, going back in time to the beautiful goddess civilizations. It is rooted in the knowledge that earth is a female planet. Mother Earth is the womb for all that lives upon her, and she has so much to teach us about the harmonies and rhythms of life, if only we would take the time to watch and listen. I am the first woman from a non-shamanic tradition to become fully initiated as a member of this society.

For people to live successfully on Earth, we must first understand and embrace the power of the sacred feminine equally and in balance with that of the sacred masculine. The women of the Sisterhood teach that to find that balance, we must understand and work with the natural forces of the entire universe, which are both male and female.

The shamanism of the Sisterhood of the Shields is the shamanism of the sacred warrioress, the spiritual warrior who knows that Mother Earth gives us life force, the life blood of our sacred body, and that the plants and animals, the four-leggeds, fish and winged ones, give us nourishment and healing both in the physical realm and in the realm of spirit as we ride the windhorse of our sacred intent into a world of harmony and light. As spiritual warriors, we do commerce in the world with the integrity of our own life and spirit. Our weapons are the shields of awareness, personal integrity, the symbols of ancient truth and the sacred give-away.

With one foot rooted firmly in the world of the physical and the other always in spirit, the spiritual warrior chooses the target carefully, takes aim, pulls back the bow and shoots the arrow with the total commitment of the warrior's spiritual and physical being. The spiritual warrior heals by looking for the patterns of dis-ease that need to be changed, much as the medicine man of the north did with Ruby. We look to Mother Earth, Father Sky and to the inner universe for guidance.

Modern civilizations have largely lost and given up our observation and intuitive understanding of Mother Earth. We've replaced it with an analytical paradigm we call 'science,' which we rely on to tell us as much as we think we need to know about the workings of the world around us. In doing so, we've placed ourselves in a peculiar sort of conundrum. Consider this: all of the animals that weren't penned-in evacuated to high ground hours in advance of the 2004 tsunami in the Indian Ocean, as did the communities of aboriginal islanders who understood what the movement of both the ocean waters and the animals meant. Because there wasn't a technological tsunami warning system in place, however, over 225,000 people in the commercial population remained at the coast and were killed.

If you step back and witness the extraordinary lifestyles that our science and technology enable us to have and then look closely at those instances where science and technology have failed us, you realize that perhaps we ought reconsider what we've really given up by losing our own powers of observation and understanding, by turning away from the knowledge and wisdom that our ancestors built over thousands and thousands of years of observing the world around them. When you move through life with a conscious awareness of earth's rhythms, you move into the flow of energy as it courses throughout the entire universe. That is when you have true power working with you and all of possibility is at your fingertips, as opposed to paddling blindly upstream the way modern people tend to do.

Think about what Mother Earth teaches us about harmonious and successful living just by observing the rhythms of her four seasonal cycles.

Spring is the time of new beginnings, when the trees bud and rains prepare the soil for new growth. For millenniums, farmers have planted their seeds with great care during the springtime so that they will weather the storms of the season that bring much needed moisture and fertilization.

Summer is the season when flowers bloom, when fruits and vegetables ripen on the vine. It is the time when farmers must tend to their crops closely, pruning away the excess growth and those branches that are not growing properly so that the life of the plant is not drained away.

Autumn is the time of harvest and reckoning as the leaves on the trees and plants begin to fall back to earth to be absorbed and transformed. It is the time when farmers harvest their crops and reap the rewards of their labor, the time when the entire community comes together.

Winter is the time when frigid temperatures send plants and animals alike deep into hibernation and dreaming in preparation for a new cycle to begin.

Think of all the honey we might extract if we were to place just earth's four seasons alongside a review of our own lives. "Beginning, middle and end," the women of the Sisterhood have said to me so many times. "Beginning, middle, and end, and then a new beginning. Life is a circle that never ends."

Individually and as a culture, we've gotten pretty good at springtime. We've gotten good at new beginnings. We've gotten so good at them, in fact, that we often fail to look at the ramifications of what we are doing. We don't look at the seeds we are going to sow and make critical decisions, such as, "Where is this going to go? Are the soils of my life fertile, or is there more I need to learn before I get started?" Instead, we get an idea and plunge right in. Then the storms come. And we discover that there were a few things that we probably should have considered before we got started. Sometimes we take so long to make a new beginning that we risk losing windows of opportunity, but, generally speaking, we humans are good at beginnings. We do it all the time.

Somewhere toward the middle, however, we tend to begin to lose interest. We become distracted, impatient, hungry for more, newer "feel-good" things. We forget all about the summertime of our projects, the critical time of cultivating and nurturing what we've planted, *even those parts of our lives that are most important to us.* When we forget to take good care of the things we start, as if they will somehow just take care of themselves, we've no business feeling picked on when they begin to fall apart. When you forget to take good care of the people in your life, relationships begin to wither. How often do you take the time to let those you love know how much you appreciate them by nurturing them in a special way?

How often do you prune and weed out that which no longer serves you, whether it is old, worn-out ideas or projects gone astray? Do you hold onto old ideas and ideologies until they strangle you? Once in a while, we make a conscious decision that something we've begun really isn't for us, and we take the steps to make some kind of reasonable closure. So much of the time, however, we lose interest and just shove things to the back shelves of our lives. Then we pile up so much unfinished business that there is no room left for ourselves, let alone for anything new and truly worthwhile.

Endings are something we don't do well in our modern world. We tend to fear and regard death as if it were the most unnatural thing in the entire universe. We've become so divorced from the concept of endings that we don't finish a great deal of what we start, with the result that we leave a trail of clutter and neglect everywhere we turn. We want to reap the rewards of what we've done, but so often we don't stay with things long enough to get there. Autumn doesn't apply to us.

As regards winter, most of us no longer recognize a period of hibernation in our lives, in winter or at any other time. Our cultures are such that we are constantly on the go. When we take a vacation, we usually fill it with so many things that we need another vacation just to recover. Even when we sleep, we expect to be back up to speed on everything that went on outside of us during those "lost" hours before we've finished our morning coffee. And then we wonder why we become so irascible and burned out?

The way we live our lives today is like if Mother Earth were to go on break half way through summer, then skip autumn and winter completely in a mad dash to get back to spring. And we wonder why we are living in greater chaos and confusion today than at any other time in human history.

When you stop to look at the catastrophic impact that our cumulative failure to understand "beginning, middle, and end" has on our lives and on this earth, you realize some things that we all need to change. In our rush to have more, bigger, better, we plunder this earth of her most important resources. We forget to take care of our infrastructures, whether they be the roads and bridges of our communities or our own bodies, until they begin to fall down around us. Our economies go through a period of growth and we think it will last forever, forgetting completely that everything in life has a beginning, a middle, and an end. We don't make provision for when the good times will wind down nor do we take the time to end things with integrity. Then, when they fall apart, we play the role of victim, "Poor me, how could this happen to *me*?"

Wherever you are in the cycles of your life, it might be a very good to have a master class with Mother Earth. Make some time to go within and take a good look at your life, where you've been and where you really want to go. Ask yourself, "Have I accomplished what I set out to do, or did I miss the mark? What did I learn from what I've just been through?" Look at your life through the energies of the four seasons and make conscious decisions about what is truly important and what you need to let go.

Then take responsibility for your world. Plant your seeds for new beginnings with great care. When you plant a seed, you are planting and cultivating energy, the energy of the life force that will send that seed on its journey toward the light so that it can blossom and become a manifested reality.

Nurture with all of your being what you are holding onto, and let go of what no longer serves you in a way that does not leave clutter. Then you will really be ready to go within, once again, to begin anew the next cycle of your life.

Do it now, when you've got the energy of the entire universe working with you. All the mysteries of the universe are there, waiting for you to discover them, just as the ancient Mayans did. Taste the honey. It is so sweet.

6

AMY HUMMINGBIRD WING II
Sisters of the Jaguar

I AWOKE THE MORNING after my time with Amy Hummingbird Wing and the *melipona* bees in a peculiar frame of mind. It was as if there was a strong sense of incompletion in my life, although I couldn't figure out why. I was there in the Yucatán with my teachers and dear friends Zoila and José Gutierrez living out my life's dream, and yet I couldn't shake the feeling that there was something missing.

"Good morning, sleepy one," Zoila said as I opened my eyes. She was sitting in a corner filled with morning sunlight, humming softly to herself as she worked on the hem of a skirt, her eyes twinkling. "It's about time you woke up. Hurry and get dressed. Amy's waiting for you."

I was surprised and excited that I would see Amy one more time, and I dressed and walked quickly down the path. When I arrived at her hut, she was gone, but she had left me a cup of a strange-smelling substance. I realized it was the sacred *balché* she had told me about, made from fermented tree bark and the first honey from the *melipona* hive and always an offering to the *melipona* god, the Descending God, *Ah-Muzen-Cab*.

After saying my prayers to the Descending God, I drank the *balchè*, thanked the spirits of place and went back outside to sit in the hammock. Almost as soon as I lay back, I fell asleep in the gently rocking hammock and a dream began to take me somewhere out into the universe, somewhere to a star that I had never before seen or been aware of, somewhere with a big forest terrain.

I suddenly found myself walking in a rainforest, feeling completely normal but at the same time knowing that I was very far away. I saw a path ahead of me and I was urged from very deep inside myself to take that path. I felt that it was the right choice, a courageous one. It was the path that, somehow, I had always studied to take.

This path was to be part of my learning. It was a magical trail. So down it I went, following it through the beautiful rainforest as I looked at the creatures, puffballs of light, strange eyes looking back at me. The earth was damp under my feet, a little slippery, and as I walked, I had to take greater and greater care not to slip.

The trail narrowed and then rose steeply and suddenly. I wondered why this was happening? I knew it was the trail I was supposed to be on, wasn't it?

With increasing difficulty, I scrambled up over rocky ground. As I took a step over the top of the trail, I suddenly realized the trail had abruptly ended. There was nowhere to go. I discovered myself to be at a dizzying height, looking down at a drop-off of thousands of feet of sheer cliff face into an ocean below. It was reminiscent of the Valley of the Kalalau on the island of Kaua'i in Hawaii, which you can get to only by kayak or by hiking the sometimes treacherous Kalalau Trail, its lush cliffs plunging 2000 feet down to the beach.

I was startled and I held onto tree branches on either side of the trail which was barely as wide as I was.

Now where do I go?

I was frightened. I didn't know where to go and I didn't know why this had happened. Moments before, I had felt very secure, sure that I knew what I was doing and where I was going. Now there was danger and I realized that I couldn't go any further. The danger was extraordinary, coming in on me like hailstones pelting into my skin. It was palpable. I started to shiver.

I turned around, not knowing what the danger was but knowing it was there, and began to backtrack. It was then that I realized there had been a fork in the trail that I hadn't even seen because it was obscured by a low hanging tree and rocks. As I backtracked to that fork in the road, I realized that I had done what I always do. I had taken the road to the right. I tend to do that, move to the right without even thinking about it. It is an aspect of me that does the same old thing as I'm going through life, the same old thing over and over again. I realized that there was a lesson here, that somehow this was to be the end of that pattern in some way.

I sat down at the fork in the trail to catch my breath, and the dream began to sway. A part of me sensed that the swaying must have been the hammock moving beneath me, gently, urging me on, but I experienced it as part of the dream.

After all, none of this is real, I thought. So I found myself walking up a new trail, and this one was very different.

I came to steps which I had to descend. At the bottom, I looked at more steps in front of me going upward, so I climbed up those steps. At their top I perched and looked down upon the floor of the forest, where I saw for the first time tens of trails going off in different directions. None of them, however, was the trail I had first taken. That one had ended before it even began.

It was no longer available to me, I thought. Part of me wanted to scramble back to that old trail because it had felt so familiar, even though it was a dead end. All these steps and all these choices of trails scared me. I realized that there were possibilities ahead of me but that I would have to make choices. I had no idea what those choices were going to be. How do you make choices about which trail to take when you don't even know where you are?

Somehow this is all a dream. It's all a dream, I kept saying. *Yes, but dreams are real.*

I heard a soft distant humming coming through the trees. I couldn't discern what was making the sound, but it was clearly some sort of humming. Was it the wind in the trees? I didn't know, but I became aware that I was going deeper now, deeper and deeper into the dream. I was completely separated from my body. I felt that my body had gone away and that I was simply in the dream body.

I looked at all the trails that lay ahead of me in the jungle and began going down the winding stairs, off the top of the pinnacle that I realized was like a pyramid, ancient and covered with growth and vines.

As I descended, I thought to myself, *How do I choose a trail?* The trails seemed to offer all possibilities to me. One was going toward a sheer mountain face with no foliage on it, jutting up out of the jungle floor. I felt a mental aspect, looking at that face of stone, granite, and lichen attached to the cliff and the sheer mountain surging upward above me.

I thought, *No, that doesn't feel right to me. Too mental, too unreasonable to go there, out of the jungle undergrowth.*

I looked at the next trail. This one was straight, like a highway, and wide enough that two of us could have walked abreast, but it was muddy, hard going, not pretty. I didn't like the fact that it wasn't pretty. There was no aesthetic to it at all. It was practical and might have taken me to wherever I was going more quickly, but I sensed that there was much I would miss that is important to me, so I chose not to take that trail, either. I looked at several more trails that forked off, but they were either so narrow or had so much foliage as to be impassible.

Finally, I came to a trail that meandered in a most elegant and graceful way, following the line of trees and flowers. Orchids hung from the trees in brilliant colors. Parrots squawked. The trail was beautiful. I chose it rather than all of the others because it afforded me beauty. I felt that the other trails which I had always taken had been so difficult. It wasn't that this trail might not be difficult, but it held up a mirror of beauty to me that spoke to something deep within me, and I so wanted to be worthy of the beauty of this trail. I wanted to be worthy of the mirror that it created for me.

I chose it knowing that my feelings about my own self-worth had created major stumbling blocks in my life many times. I felt that in this trail, however, there was an added aspect of inspiration, that, somehow, the Great Spirit was calling me to follow it. I knew not where it went nor what was ahead of me, but I felt grounded in the teaching that the old trails, perhaps, no longer worked for me, that now I was to take a new trail, one I couldn't describe or map out but a trail that, nevertheless, would afford me great opportunity even though it was part of the unknown.

All at once I felt the dream shattering. The hammock on which I was sleeping swung from one side to the other. I was brought back sharply into the present and flung onto the ground, landing on my face. I lay there for a few moments. What had happened?

Suddenly, Amy Hummingbird Wing was there, putting her arms around me, turning me over and helping me sit up.

"What happened? What happened?" I asked. It was an extraordinary shock. I felt sick to my stomach and leaned over, rocking back and forth, trying to get my consciousness into some sort of reality. I shook my head. Amy gave me some tea.

"Just sip a little at a time," she said, massaging my back between my shoulder blades. I couldn't move. I just rocked back and forth. I couldn't stand up. It was okay. I didn't mind sitting there. I didn't mind letting time pass.

I started to move back into the dream, but caught myself. I was shaking a bit. My hands felt numb. I wondered what had happened to me and I didn't care. I kept seeing the trails forking out into the distance, into the jungle, wondering if maybe I had taken the wrong fork.

I looked at Amy and asked, "Did I take the wrong trail? Did I take the wrong path?"

She laughed, smiling broadly, and said, "It's a simple lesson, my dear, my little one. Don't you see? It's a simple, simple lesson. You were in danger when we began. You were in great danger."

"But how? What do you mean?" I asked, as she helped me to my feet. I didn't want to stand, but I did. She guided me into the hut and I sat down on some blankets.

"Shush," she said and made some sounds under her breath in her native language. She spoke such broken English to me that sometimes I couldn't understand her. But I could understand the gesture and the intent in her mind through the movements of her hands and arms. She took a tortilla, placed it in a heated flat pan and put pieces of cactus and cheese on it. Then she wrapped it and gave it to me to eat.

It was so good. I couldn't eat it fast enough. I felt like I had been in a marathon. When I was through eating, I wiped my mouth and my fingers with a piece of cloth woven in blues and yellows that Amy gave me.

"Here," she said, "wipe your hands. Wipe your face." I realized that I had the tortilla and its contents all over my face.

Finally, after I was a bit revived, Amy lit several candles and burned some copal in an abalone shell. The pungent aroma filled the hut, encircling me in smoke, like a snake.

"Now, tell me," she said.

"I went into a deep dream, and I was walking down a path that I chose out of several. It seemed so easy."

"What did it look like?" she asked.

"Well, it was beautiful at first, with trees and agave plants, then taller trees and cactus. And then it became a path of steps up a mountain. I was struggling. Then, before I knew it, I was on a narrow plateau and I almost fell over a ledge."

She handed me a stick that had been worked. There had been many hands on this stick long before mine. They were skilled and had carved tiny symbols onto one end of it. There was a jaguar head at the top, beautifully carved out of the cream-colored wood. I ran my fingers over the figures and enjoyed the feel of them. I realized that she wanted me to understand something. She spoke in Quiché, which I could not understand.

Then she took a small hunting knife out of her scabbard. She had another stick with her and she whittled on it for a few minutes, scraping little chips onto the earthen floor of the hut. I looked at the ceiling, the *lattias* placed perfectly on the roof between the *vigas*, large beams of bamboo or wood that have elbows and joints in them. I looked around the hut. It had clay and some boards, and I noticed that there were pieces of a car. The sides of a pickup truck had been nailed into one side of the hut. It was beautiful and primitive, and I felt at home.

Maybe it reminded me of Agnes's cabin, the first time I ever saw it. There were gatherings of dried herbs and grasses hanging over one side of the doorway where the sun would come in and dry the sprigs more quickly. Mexican *serapés* were over the bed, one with green that I just loved. I kept thinking that I had better not say that I liked it because Amy would surely give it to me, and I felt that she needed it. There were clay pots filled with what I imagined was honey, sitting on the floor. Everything, the pots, the very primitive, single-walled dwelling with light coming through the cracks, made a play of shadows on the floor like Hopi dancers in ceremony around a fire.

It was wonderful, and I settled down, centering myself, and praying for a moment for Great Spirit to give me the wisdom and the strength to learn. I opened my eyes and Amy was staring at me, her face serious, her skin lined with what looked like a thousand years of experience and sun. Her character was beautiful and empowering to me.

She stopped whittling, set her stick down, and pointed the knife at the stick that I held.

"Do you know what that is?" she asked.

I looked at it and said, "Well, it must be some kind of a jaguar stick."

"Yes," she said, not smiling.

I was getting a little nervous. I was feeling a tinge of discomfort, maybe even fright.

"Tell me about this stick. Use yourself," she said.

I took a deep breath and I began to feel along the length of stick as I held it between my knees. "This reminds me of a talking stick."

"How is that?" she asked.

"Well," I said as I rubbed back and forth, "there's a sticky place here toward the end where the jaguar is, but before all the other little niches and carving. A talking stick has this same thing." It wasn't sticky from any substance. It was the stick, itself, holding my fingers, drawing my attention to that place. I felt some more. Definitely it was that spot.

"This is the heart of this stick."

She smiled and said, "Yes, it is. The fingers of many who have gone before you have held this stick. It is an honor, and I don't give it to just anyone to hold. So, little one, I honor you. Your heart and my heart beat with the heart of the jaguar stick. We are blessed to be able to experience this."

"But what is it used for?" I asked.

"It is used to measure your wealth."

"My wealth?" I said not quite knowing what she meant. "Do you mean money?"

Amy laughed. "Oh, all you white people think of is money. No, no, no I mean the wealth of your spirit. You have dreamed, and you have dreamed with me. You have gone to the paths of the forked trail. Those paths have been traversed for centuries by warriors of spirit, as you are. It is a simple lesson, but an important one."

I took the stick and held it up to the light, now dimming, and to the candlelight.

It must be very late, I thought. Or maybe it was morning. I looked at the tiny carvings and said, "You know, if I were to carve on this stick, I would put a dot right here, just below the jaguar's mouth." Suddenly my surroundings began to mist away. All I saw was the jaguar face on the end of the stick. My eyes opened wide as the face carved in wood shape-shifted and became a real jaguar. Her eyes stared into mine, and then, as if she were playing with her cub, she licked my cheek and was gone. I looked around, my heart pounding. My fingers caressed the wetness on my cheek. I had the most profound opening in my heart. Tears filled my eyes in wonderment. I knew there was nothing to say—Amy had seen it all.

She looked at me for a little bit, reaching her palms out toward my body but not touching me. She moved her hands around me, feeling my energy field, not saying anything. She began to sing very softly, as she had to the bees. I could hear the bees, what sounded like a hoard of them circling above us. As she ended the song, the bees flew away. I was startled and waited for

what was next. Amy startled me by taking out an awl with a very
sharp end which had been tucked inside her sash.

"You dreamed well," she said as I recovered. "I am proud of
you. Oftentimes, it takes six or seven days for someone to dream
as you did, without the help of the vine of death or the sacred
cactus drink. You traveled and you learned the lesson. When you
went down the first trail and you came to that cliff, what did you
feel?" She took the awl and put the point of it into the flame of a
candle, getting it hot.

"Well, I felt terrified."

"It's okay to be scared. Fear is a good thing. It often awakens
you to harm."

"But why was I in danger?" That was what I didn't understand.

"You were in danger because you kept taking the same trails
over and over again. You were like a mouse in a maze, digging for
food in the same little holes, trying to find something new but
staying on the same trail."

I realized that I had been following a very similar thread all
of my life, searching for knowledge, always searching, curious,
voraciously hungry for learning but not knowing where to look.

She said, "You did have the presence of mind not to fall down
that cliff thinking it was the only trail to take, which would have
been at your absolute peril. If you had even tried to crawl down
that cliff, it would have been your demise. Instead, you crawled
back down the side of the trail you had taken up. You didn't give
up and try to go home. You went back to the fork and looked at
the other trails. You waited. You felt in your power center, around
your navel, where the first dream is, the first original mind, and
you listened to it. Even though you were in the dream, you listened to it. You found the trail that was beautiful for you.

"And it is a different thread," she said, reading my mind, making me feel even more uncomfortable. "So you see, if you take the same trail always, you become a warrior in great danger because you're not learning anything and it will kill you. Instead, you found another path, a true path, a shift in consciousness, and you saved yourself and came back to me."

"Yes, but why did you spill me onto the ground?"

"Oh, I didn't," she said. "That was your choice."

"It was not! I just found myself face down in the dirt."

"No. You struggled. You struggled with yourself. In a sense, I don't think you wanted to come back yet. But you needed to. You can only stay out so long," she said.

Now, the point of the awl that she was holding in her hand had gotten red hot. The sunlight had dimmed through the slits in the walls and the firelight had become much more brilliant in the growing darkness.

"Here," she said. "Take this." And she put the handle in my hand. "Now, put your dot on the jaguar stick, right where you said."

I looked at her in wonderment, thinking, *Are you sure?*

"Yes, I am sure," she said.

Placing the stick on the ground and holding it very securely, I placed the point of the awl where I wanted it to be and there was a sizzling, as if I had lit sage or copal. Smoke came and then, as I held it there, more and more smoke, much more than you would imagine for such a small stick and such a small effort. I pulled the awl away from the stick.

She said, "Now, breathe deeply of the smoke."

I did. It relaxed me so. She held out her hand and I held it. She said, "Now, Little Wolf, we are sisters. We are sisters of the jaguar. Your dreams will be many, but they will be teaching dreams. I bless you."

She gave me some honey to take with me and put the jaguar stick into a beautiful woven bag, obviously very sacred to her. She said good-bye to me as I walked back again on a trail toward Zoila's. I was so sad to leave her, and yet, when the teachings are finished, it is important to respect that. Again, as if reading my mind she nodded her head, touched her heart, turned around and walked in the opposite direction.

Circling Back: "Shape-Shifting in an Ever-Changing World"

When I boarded the plane in Merida to fly home to Beverly Hills after my time with Amy and Zoila, I felt like I had a foot in two worlds. I wondered about the bees and the dream I had on the second day with Amy. I reached my fingers to my ear and felt the earring that she had given me, its polished silver, in the *milagra* form of a jaguar. Instantly I was back in her hut with the smell of wood and copal smoke. Amy's face appeared in front of me, smiling and bright.

The flight attendant asked me if I wanted something to drink and I jerked back into the present. As I sipped my orange juice, I thought back on my early studies of the Mayan culture. I thought of my experiences with these contemporary women of such strong Mayan heritage as visions of powerful shamans magically transforming into jaguars danced before me. I know that I was doubly blessed, to have these experiences in the first place and to be so open to receiving the wisdom and sense of knowing they helped me to find.

"Shape-shifting." What do you think that means?

Modern people look at shape-shifting as the mysterious and highly improbable invention of sorcerers and magicians, drawn from the mythical beliefs of a "primitive" people trying to understand the world without the benefit of science and the modern way of thinking.

I am here to tell you, however, that shape-shifting is very, very real. It is the real ability of highly skilled shamans across the earth who understand how energy moves and how to choreograph that energy to a very high degree. I have seen it with my own eyes. I have experienced it in my own soul.

I am also here to tell you that shape-shifting is something that you and I and every other person on the face of this earth have the innate ability to do. More than that, it is a beautiful and powerful way of seeing and living in an all-too-real world that is fraught with disorder.

One evening in the Yucatán, Agnes, Ruby, Zoila, myself and several local women were sitting around a small fire in the jungle. We had recently done ceremony and we were talking, sharing stories and doing wonderful things together in the most simple of ways.

All of a sudden Zoila stood up and began to gather her energy. I could see her centering herself. She began circling around the fire in a clockwise fashion, which is the direction energy moves around earth. She turned to look at each of us in the eyes, and then suddenly she turned her back and took on the shape of a jaguar, which is her power animal. She snarled a wild scream and looked at us as if we were prey, bounding around the fire and then leaping out of the hut, leaving us absolutely spellbound. It was a spectacular example of someone shape-shifting right before my eyes, and I was stunned.

I am very much a 21st century woman of Western culture. Although I had heard my teachers speak of what Zoila had just done, I had never seen it and, frankly, I was skeptical. Now I sat there and could not move. After a while, those of us still sitting began to talk. Zoila was gone for several hours. When she returned, she was back in her human form, but we could see on the earthen floor the paw marks of the jaguar where she had been circling the fire. She came in and sat down with us, as if nothing had occurred.

Then she began to talk about shape-shifting. Earlier that day we had been talking about the different ways our own cultures experience disease. I told them how difficult it is for my culture to accept the diagnosis of serious, what we consider "catastrophic," illness, such as heart disease or cancer, which we experience in record numbers. To us, there is almost a belief in the inevitability of an early death even being born into a family with a history of such diseases because, "That's what my family does. They die an early death from heart disease," or diabetes, for example.

These women of the Yucatán couldn't imagine why our culture chooses to suffer from disease the way we do. Zoila commented, "Why in the world would anyone choose that dream to live in? Why would you not choose the dream of health, instead? I cannot imagine why your people, who come down to teach us about your world, actually have so little to teach us. We have so much to teach you."

Then she said, "Don't you understand that you don't have to choose a dream of suffering or war? You can choose a dream of well-being. You can choose a dream of success. You can choose a dream of health. Why would you do otherwise? I am healthy. Why isn't everybody else healthy?"[1]

The women of the Sisterhood of the Shields are dumbstruck by our "modern"condition because we choose to allow ourselves to live in a state of consciousness where disease, war, and all the other perils of our societies have a chance to prosper and to grow. It is a conscious choice that we make. These conditions thrive

---

1   From *Jaguar Woman.* ©1985, by Lynn Andrews.

precisely because we believe in them. We believe in their power over us. We believe in their "inevitability" and, because of our beliefs, we take actions that fuel their onset. If you come from a family with a history of heart disease, the chances are that you, also, may have a weakness in this area. But that weakness doesn't mean that you will develop heart disease. And if you do develop heart disease, it doesn't mean that you will die from it at an early age. It doesn't mean that your life has to be defined by your heart disease, that you have to have your vitality and your joy, your creativity in this world consumed by the fear of an early death.

The world in which my teachers live also has heart disease, cancer, broken bones, all of the perils of life. But the people don't live in the grip of these hardships. They aren't weakened to the point of paralysis by the "inevitability" of anything. As a result, they don't experience the potentiality of these conditions at anywhere near the rate that we do in our societies. They know that if people change their attitude toward disease and change their belief structure about it, they may still be fragile in that part of their bodies, but now they can put themselves in the position of strength in living with it.

This is the reality of shape-shifting. If you are someone who believes that for whatever the reason you don't have the possibility of having a happy, successful, and healthy life, doing things that you love to do, then you probably won't have a happy, successful, and healthy life doing things that you love to do. But if you can change your mind-set about the possibilities that life holds for you, then you can change what needs to be changed to alter the dreary course of your life. You shape-shift out of a person who is vulnerable to cancer, for example, into a person who chooses health and wellness. You shape-shift out of a person who was born to poverty into a person who welcomes abundance into your life . You do this by changing your belief structure about things like disease, poverty, war, and their power over you. You change your belief structure about your own self-worth and you shape-shift from a person who has no future into a person with endless possibilities in life!

Shape-shifting comes from the heart, not the mind, especially when you are speaking about your physical and spiritual health. With the expression of your heart and your feeling, envision what you want. You want to have better health! You want to be a successful writer, a happy mother, a leader in your community! This is your heartfelt dream. So why, then, are you living out a dream where you are ill, where you haven't even begun all of the great things you are really capable of doing and being?

It is when you change the energy of your thoughts that possibility begins. Zoila told me that the important thing to see is that when she turns into a jaguar, she is a jaguar. She has changed her energy to the energy of the jaguar. She knows how to do that because she understands the oneness that all of life represents. She does not believe herself to be separate from the jaguar, because she knows that they are both part of the noble Oneness that comes from the Great Spirit. The first lesson of power is that we are all alone. The final lesson of power is that we are all one.

Western culture believes in separation far more than Oneness. Most Westerners would seek to control the jaguar or perhaps even eliminate it because we are afraid of it. In this way, we have driven countless majestic beings to the brink of extinction, four-legged, finned, and winged ones who are teachers for us of how to live successfully on this earth, in harmony and peace with our environment rather than at war against it. We do not have the right to do this, nor is it even close to necessary.

The shaman, on the other hand, says, "Become the jaguar. Then, in that oneness, see the amazing realm of possibility that lies before you!"

This is the way of the shape-shifter, and to the shaman it is what life is all about. We come here to learn, little by little, how to become a total human being, free from the kinds of ideas and imperfections that bring us to a place of suffering and dis-ease.

Everything we see in life is made out of energy. When you realize and accept this in a conscious way—that no matter what is before you, it is all about energy rather than form—then you begin to realize just how completely your thoughts, which are energy, give form to your energy body *and to* your physical body. Then you can truly see how you have supported whatever weakness you may be carrying in your genetic make-up. Did you know you can change that make-up? Yes, you certainly can, and it begins with changing the way you think about things like "inevitability."

Life can be whatever dream you want it to be. That is why my teachers ask, "Why on earth would anyone choose such a negative dream as war or the inevitability of illness?"

The reality of shape-shifting comes through your heart, not your mind. When you see pictures of the jaguar, when you watch documentaries or have the fabulous opportunity of seeing one in the wild, your heart is warmed by its magnificence, by the lithe gracefulness of the way it moves, the power of its being. It is the mind that tells you scary stories about it. Your heart tells you, "How extraordinary. How exquisite. How like you."

Realize the magnificence that you are and make that your focus, not the possibility that you are carrying weak genes that might manifest in debility if you think about it enough. Then shape-shift yourself into the truly wonderful person you are meant to be.

7

CRYSTAL MOUNTAIN DREAMING

I KEPT SMELLING COPAL smoke coming from somewhere in the distance. I was in a deep sleep and I woke up in my dreaming enough to know that I had to dream further. That is to say, I knew I was, somehow or other, meant to be sleeping. There was spiritual work to be done.

Again I fell out of memory, following with my senses the copal smoke that seemed to be drifting around me. I felt secure, the same way I had felt when I was swaying gently in Amy Hummingbird Wing's hammock, comfortable and at ease. As I followed the scent of the copal, I could begin to taste the sweetness of honey lingering in my mouth. Although asleep, I realized that within my dreaming, I was feeling as I had when I was with Amy. This is not an uncommon experience in our dreams, although often we don't remember it upon waking because it feels so unusual that our rational minds don't want to think about it. If you have been out of body in your dreaming, it can be difficult to come back because it is jarring, and sometimes it even hurts.

I followed the smoke into a mirage of mountains and crystal-covered peaks, strange-looking and unidentifiable. I kept floating in and out of this mirage until, going much deeper into my sleep, I felt a sudden "whoosh," a gravity pull to the mountains where I walked on a trail, mist around my feet.

I couldn't really see the ground, but I knew where to go. Then up ahead of me was a mirror-like piece of mica on the mountain. I was drawn to it. As I approached it, I began to see moving reflections that looked like shutters of an old film. I felt encouraged to sit and watch these images playing out on the pieces of mica.

As I sat there, fascinated, I began to see pictures of my early life, pictures of one experience after another moving into darkness and swirling clouds of emotions, pictures of sobbing and laughter. It was as I would imagine the *bardo* in Buddhism to be, the intermediate state after death that occurs when awareness is first freed from the body.

I was seeing reflection after reflection of my mother, her beauty, her sadness. I saw the separation of me from her for a couple of years when I was young, the abandonment and all of the things that we feel in our early emotions. But there was no reasoning, no thinking that "*I shouldn't* have done this" or "*I should* have done that." It was just pictures of the experiences that I had gone through, without judgment. I don't know how long I stayed in my dreaming, but the whole of my life flashed before me in picture after picture.

As I was approaching the period of my life now, a being of light rose out of the mica. She was Mountain Spirit Woman. She was of the mountain and the mountain was of her. She wore sparkling garments. A "fairy queen" would be an apt description. Her hair was long, and she was young. She was also watching me intently.

At first, I was afraid of her because I knew instantly that she saw the truth of me. I have looked at the truth of me and expressed it many times in my work with the Sisterhood, yet there was, in the first moments of the encounter with this great being of light, a foreboding, a feeling of intense terror.

She held out her arms toward me, never touching me. Still the pictures were going by behind her. I was so entranced by them that I barely realized that Mountain Spirit Woman had come over to stand beside me. Then I felt her warmth. At the same time as I looked into her eyes, the pictures stopped coming. I had reached present time in my history.

She held in her hands the *Book of the Child* which I had seen before, in the Valley of Luktang when I was in Tibet with Ani and the Sisterhood of the Shields. She began speaking to me.

"You have been seeing in pictures what is written in the *Book of the Child*," she said. As she spoke, the pictures flashed again over the mica and, in a great whirling "whoosh," went onto or into the pages of the *Book of the Child*, my history, my present and past lives.

I said, "Does this also include future lives? And who are you? You are so beautiful."

She said, in the sweetest voice, "Do not be afraid. This activity is not a punishment. It is a marker in your approach to understanding this life and the highest awareness to which you could arrive. This is how the Sisterhood sees you. We can see through this experience what more you need to learn in this lifetime."

"Are you part of our circle?" I asked?

"I know you don't recognize me," she answered. "You have met all the women in the Sisterhood of the Shields. I was once incarnate for a long time in your history on this earth. I have chosen, now, to work on other levels of consciousness."

She laughed and I saw for a moment a way that Amy Hummingbird Wing had laughed with me. Then it faded, instantly.

She continued. "Many times we choose to come back, as you know, to experience things that give us strength in our spirit shields. This experience is essential for you."

"What is it that I need to learn?" I asked.

She laughed and said, "Well, a few things."

Then I was frightened. I didn't know where this would lead me, where it might drop me off. Eventually, after some time of our just sitting together, Mountain Spirit Woman brought up pictures of my mother and me. There was a picture of us standing in our apartment in Brentwood when I was in high school. We were discussing what I wanted to do with my life. At that time, I had said something like, "Maybe I could be a secretary or secretarial assistant, like you are." Without thinking, my mother had said, "Well, you have to be smart to do that," which to a high school girl implied that I was not smart enough and I said so to Mom, but the damage had been done. It had hurt me deeply.

"I don't know if I ever recovered from that," I said to Mountain Spirit Woman.

"Yes, that is the question," she said. "I want you to hold my hand." As I did, it felt like I was holding my mother's hand and it instantly made me cry. I felt my mother and missed her so. I remembered again that moment, *"You have to be smart to do that."*

I knew that I was smart, but that was the first time I had doubted it. I had kept trying to find my IQ scores at my school. I remembered wondering why in the world this was happening? I had been called a genius, told I had a genius IQ. Why would my mother say this to me? Maybe they had been lying to me. I guess it didn't matter.

"What matters," Mountain Spirit Woman said, "is how you feel about your own intelligence and accomplishments. This is not a complicated matter. It is a matter of you coming to terms with how you fight yourself."

"What do you mean, 'fight yourself?'"

"When you start to do something, there is a voice inside you that says, 'I can't do this; I'm not good enough.' Is that not correct?"

I thought for a little while. "Yes, that has been part of my exhaustion."

"Yes, it is part of your exhaustion. You are exhausted because you don't know, truly, if you are strong enough. The problem is that you fight yourself. You do not feel that you are powerful, and yet you act in a powerful way. That creates a stress. You know that you're okay, but underneath it all, you don't really believe it and you won't let yourself *feel* alright. That's what so many of your sisters and brothers do, as well. It's part of what you've come here to learn."

"What do you mean?"

"Well, this world that we live in is a schoolhouse, this great earth. You know that. It's a schoolhouse for your spirit. Haven't you ever wondered why this is happening to you? Don't you ever wonder?"

"What do you mean, a schoolhouse? I don't want to go through this anymore. I know it's a schoolhouse. Sometimes I get so tired of this. I get so tired of constantly having to learn and to grow. I'm not sure I want to go through this any more."

Mountain Spirit Woman lashed at me and said, "We have all felt that way so many times. But you know as well as I do that we have one intent, and one intent only, on this earthwalk. And that is to learn what we came here to learn."

Slowly her light diminished. Her eyes smiled at me as she turned and walked off into the mountain, disappearing in the clouds that had gathered around us as we spoke. The clouds looked like a city of gold with high spires of light and dark canyons of thunder and lightning. I thought she turned again to look at me, but then I realized it was as if she had become a spire of golden clouds.

We get so locked into a cycle of fighting with ourselves endlessly, to the point that it drains us of all vitality and life force. It kills our passion and desire to fulfill our dreams. Mountain Spirit Woman reminded me that when I feel like that, it is a choice I make. She reminded me that I know what my purpose in this life is. I know the great dream for my life, and I know that when I fight against myself, it gets me nowhere. I am so thankful that my teachers have shown me how to go into the dreamtime to remember who I am, so that I can break out of self-destructive ways.

Yes, it was time for spiritual work to be done. Our dreams have the power to show us that, when we learn how to listen to them.

Circling Back: "Dreaming, A Shaman's Perspective"

Several years ago, I had the opportunity to apprentice with a healer named Ginevee, an Aboriginal woman of high degree in the Australian Outback, who is a member of the Sisterhood of the Shields.

Much of our work together was about "dreaming," the sacred practice of a people that is tens of thousands of years old. This dreaming is central to Aboriginal belief and understanding of life, how the universe and the Earth came into being, what the origins of their land and their ancestors are, how the Creator gods and goddesses intend for people to live.

Aboriginal people believe that the world was originally conceived in the dreamtime, a mythology which informs every aspect of their lives: their laws, their spirituality, how they use the land, and their taboos. Aboriginal people born today will explore the dreamtime in much the same way as their ancestors did, and their ancestors before them, through sacred dreaming and the oral traditions of their people. This is how they learn about their sacred selves.

Ginevee did not teach me Aboriginal dreaming, nor about their customs, the people, or their sacredness, nor did she teach me how to enter their dreamtime, and I do not teach it in my work with others. What she taught me is how to approach dreaming as a conscious activity with all of the power of my own sacred intent, how to transcend the boundaries of my conscious mind *in a conscious, intended way* in order to explore the deeper truths and meanings to my life.

Throughout history and across the world, shamans everywhere have always considered dreaming to be a conscious activity, not an unconscious one. It is the bridge to a higher consciousness in every aspect of life. Through my work with shaman women from cultures as diverse as the Australian Outback, Nepal, the far north of Canada, the Mayan Yucatán, and Guatemala, I have learned that conscious dreaming is one of the great universals that is shared by peoples of shamanic tradition, everywhere.

Nobody owns the truth, just as nobody owns God, the Great Spirit, the divine harmony and the essence of life. There are many different and wonderful spiritual pathways which embrace so many of the same teachings, just expressed in different ways. All of them lead, I believe, to the same place, the place where we are one with Great Spirit and all that is in the universe, the place within ourselves where we are One with all of life.

Conscious dreaming is a practice that is accessible to anyone, anywhere in the world, if you are willing to work at it. It does not matter whether you have been raised in a shamanic culture that considers dreaming to be as fundamental to life as breathing or in the Western tradition, where dreaming is so often relegated to what our minds do to entertain themselves while our bodies rest. When you practice conscious dreaming, you learn to go into your dreams to learn about your sacred self—how you think, how your emotions grow as you move towards enlightenment.

It can sometimes be very difficult for people in the Western world to understand so many of the aspects which are central to a shamanic understanding of life because we have no frame of reference either in our experience or our language. English is a very pragmatic language. It is strongly based in the practical world of commerce and science, just as Western civilization is more grounded in the fast-paced external world than the intuitive, spirit-based world of a shamanic culture.

Dreaming is one of those areas where our language fails us in our understanding of the possibilities that life holds.

In the Aboriginal world, dreaming helps the people to define their world view. In English, we usually talk about "dreaming" when we are talking about the thoughts, images, and emotions that our mind conjures up to entertain itself while our body is sleeping, while we are in a state of unconsciousness rather than consciousness.

We also use the word "dream" to explain the creations of our imagination, which we then look at as rather childish, even though everything that we do begins somewhere in our imagination. We use the word "dream" when we talk about our daydreams, which we so often consider to be those flights of fantasy that give us a brief respite from the pressures of our world, something that isn't real but is nonetheless a nice break from reality. I do believe, however, that the Wright brothers would heartily disagree with you if you were to say to them that their daydreams were not real! Always remember this, if you can dream it, you can do it.

And we use "dream" when we talk about our vision, as in our hope for a better world, something that may be beyond our grasp but still a nice "dream."

There is no sense of the word "dream" in our contemporary language that connotes transcending the boundaries of the known world and our own conscious minds in an intentional way in order to enter a higher realm of consciousness to gather information. In fact, there are a lot of people who would tell you that such an endeavor is pure fantasy.

Shamanic dreaming is exactly about learning to transcend the boundaries of your conscious mind in a conscious, intended way and it has been practiced by totally sane people all over the world for millenniums. It is a state of consciousness that nearly everyone who has ever lived has experienced at one time or another, although in our culture we usually do not realize it when it happens, and so we tend either to ignore or discount as fantasy the images and information that come to us.

You can enter into a state of conscious dreaming in a couple of different ways. Carlos Castaneda wrote about it extensively in his work with his teacher, Don Juan Matus, through the use of selected hallucinogens, and he was stunned when Don Juan told him that he could have accomplished the same thing without using any drugs. My teachers did not use drugs in their work with me, and I never use them. Once in a while you may encounter in my writings the ceremonial uses of certain plants and herbs that the Sisterhood has occasionally used in sacred ritual, but they are few and far between.

The Sisterhood taught me a series of chants, sounds, breath work, and focused concentration to relax my mind and body so that I can move beyond the limits of my conscious mind and enter other worlds, other realms of consciousness in such a way that I am able to interact with the beings I meet there and remember my experiences when I come back into my conscious mind. Modern people sometimes refer to this as having an "out of body" experience and, indeed, when I am in the dreamtime I am not aware of my physical body. Rather, the whole of my consciousness is in another realm altogether, although I, Lynn Andrews, continue to breathe in my own body and it is to my own body that I return when I come out of the dreaming.

When you learn conscious dreaming, you move to a higher level of spirituality, a higher understanding of your own sacredness and the role which sacredness plays in your life. You learn to trust the messages as well as the messengers, the spirits of the ancestors and sacred beings that you meet who give you information that will help you in your daily life. You learn to walk with one foot planted firmly in the physical world and one foot in the world of spirit in order to become whole and healed within yourself.

Through conscious dreaming, you rediscover the magic of your original nature, who you truly are in this world and what the great dream is for your own life. It is actually about waking up from the dream world of illusion created by all of the conditioning, fears, and distractions that anesthetize us and finding yourself in the very real dream of your own sacred truth.

8

TWIN DREAMERS

"Everything has been written by the gods. All things considered within our lifetime have been written in the *Book of the Child*," said Twin Dreamers.

She and I were sitting by a fire on a mountain top in southern Mexico. A little bit earlier, it had been cold, that time of year when the frost sometimes comes early and the earth and all living things go into hibernation, into a different kind of thoughtfulness when the light slants across the land and leaves long shadows. At the moment, however, it was beautiful, with shards of light streaking through the trees. In the distance, heavy rain clouds were beginning to swirl. Looking at them, Twin Dreamers winked at me and said, ""Storm coming."

Yes, storm coming, I thought looking at her. We both knew that she was referring to an old friend I had not seen in many years. Yet there was a look in her eyes that was so penetrating I knew it was filled with unspoken meaning. Oftentimes, she would say nothing, and yet I understood her meaning.

"You are looking at me in a way that I have never seen," I said.

Twin Dreamers got up quickly, with great agility, and began to circle around me, first to the right and then to the left. I tried to keep my eyes on her, but it was almost impossible. She would climb up in a tree and then jump down and go around to the other side. She would sit back on her haunches for a moment and then spring up and go the other way around. I started to laugh, because her movements were so comical and disjointed. It was not graceful, like she can so often be. It was very disconcerting, and all I could do was laugh. I lost my train of thought and giggled, watching her.

"What are you doing?" I asked.

"What does it look like I'm doing?"

"You're jumping and running around in circles and distracting me."

She nodded her head. "Yep."

I settled myself a little deeper into my heart and we began to speak.

"Twin Dreamers, we've been together a long time, longer, perhaps, than I ever will remember."

She looked at me quizzically, sitting in a fork in the branches of a tree.

"What are you thinking?" she asked. Then, laughing hysterically, she asked, "Do you feel like a tree that is dropping its leaves?"

"Not exactly," I said, trying to find my focus. "But I am surrounded by my memories. I am filled with the joy of having been fortunate to have lived my life doing what I love to do, living my passion, but I feel like my life is still way ahead of me, that I have only begun my journey."

She began to twist her long tendrils of gray hair. At times, she could look very unkempt, yet I knew that she was one of the cleanest, most fastidious people in the world. She had a way, however, of looking the opposite of that.

"You know what I want to do?" I said.

"What's that?" she said, still twisting her hair.

"I want to talk to you about what you feel about life. I'm tired of hearing myself talk about my experiences. All of you in the Sisterhood have lived with me through my frailties, through my strengths, through everything, all my sadness and grief. Now I want to hear about yours. Would you do that for me? Would you talk to me about what it is that you see we human beings need in this world?"

She cleared her throat, as if to begin a great soliloquy, looking suddenly elegant perched on her branch.

"Well, it's like this." She waited a few moments, her eyes gleaming. "It was a dark and stormy night," and then she shrieked with laughter. I laughed with her because that had been a kind of standing joke with us for years. She knew all of the times I had been nearly scared out of my wits during my early work with the Sisterhood; she had been there through much of it.

Finally serious, she said, "I like to speak of the essence of things. We get lost in our physical lives. Your people, your dear, wonderful people, are so filled with stress and consternation. With all your institutions of higher learning, your people still don't know what they are doing on the most simple, basic foundations of life. You have it all in your hands, like treasures of gold, but you don't see it. Your insistence on control and war is beyond my imagination and my ability to handle the sadness that it causes me."

All of a sudden big tears welled up in her eyes. She leapt down from the tree, landing on my right, near me. She picked up an old *serapé* with streaks of orange, green, and yellow in its weave and wrapped it around herself, even though it wasn't particularly cold.

"But I don't want to talk about war," she said. "I don't want to talk about that horrible dream, which is so easy for us to get caught in." Her tears had dried and I watched as she lifted out of

her physical body to a higher awareness. I have seen this transformation so often in all of these women. I have experienced it
myself, and I teach others how to do it. Yet it is always such a
profound experience to witness a person of high degree shift the
entire nature of her being.

Putting down the *serapé*, she moved to a flat rock nearby and
sat down. She had on jeans that came half way up her calves, a
white blouse embroidered with blue, red, and yellow figures of
animals, and a beautifully woven sash tied around her waist with
long ties hanging down. The sash had been made on a backstrap
loom from Guatemala. It looked similar to the *ecot* weavings of
Indonesia where the colors blend into each other.

I had never seen her dressed like this before. Her long hair
usually made her look like she could have been a crazy woman,
and I think that was exactly what she wanted people to think. She
loved it and laughed when people would look at her strangely.
On this fine day, however, she had on long earrings, and the sun
was gleaming off silver discs that hung down below her chin. She
was shaking her head and I wondered if she was enjoying the feel
of the earrings against her face.

In nearly perfect English with an accent almost impossible
to trace, she said, "I was born in this lifetime." She took a stone
out of the pocket of her jeans, held it and gently rubbed it with
her thumb. The stone was very shiny and fit into the palm of
her hand. As she rubbed it, she closed her eyes and went to her
place of second attention, a state of consciousness that is above
ordinary consciousness. This attention is where you go when you
create a painting, a book, when you move into a place where you
find yourself communicating with the energies in the universe
in a way that is different from your every-day consciousness. She
began to speak to me very quietly and quite slowly.

"I was born a long time ago in a small tribe in the Panama jungle, and I was very, very lucky." She kept rubbing her stone as she spoke, and every once in a while she would rub it against her cheek and then return it to the palm of her hand.

"The tribe raised me. I had not only one mother, I had ten mothers and ten fathers, and if one mother was busy and I needed attention, there was always another mother there. That is the beauty of being raised by a tribe of people. You sleep together, you eat together. Everything is done together. And if you want to be by yourself, you can do that, too. People watch over you, they care for you and they love you. There is constant affection one way or another, and I guess that is one of the reasons it is hard for me, and sad, as well, to see that your people are raised separately. They live separately, and if two parents work there is no one to be home for the children. I grew up playing and was excited about my life. I would sleep in the same hammock as my mother and father, snuggled up between them. I could go from one hammock to another if I wanted, but I didn't do that much.

"There was one thing about this tribe that I forgot to tell you. It was really a tribe of shamans. Each and every person in that tribe had his or her ability to travel through dreams, to manifest something like you have spoken about Sai Baba in India who manifests trinkets and objects in his hands and gives them to you as gifts. We are very skilled in healing the mind and the heart. We learned to play games with those who need healing to help them open their vision and see something new and different. Sometimes we do unexpected things, like climbing up into trees or looking very strange, the opposite of what one would expect, to shock people out of their dis-eased way of looking at things. That is when healing can begin to happen.

"These were shaman people who had learned from their ancestors of the Olmec, people from very, very ancient tradition.

The Olmecs are all gone now, and they have never really been written about. We know about them because they left magnificent, very unusual carvings and statues. I would walk into a field and find a great head carved out of stone, perfectly and beautifully shaped. It would just be sitting there. I would sit with these Olmec heads and wonder bout them. I would touch them, run my fingers over the smooth surfaces, wondering who had made them and how long they had been there.

"And then one day, a woman, an older woman, well, actually, she was young but she seemed old to me then!" Twin Dreamers stopped talking, threw her head back and laughed, watching my face. I was laughing, too. It is so true. When you are young, everybody seems so much older. As you get older, everybody seems younger, including yourself. You want to be as you have always been. Then she began talking about this woman.

"The woman was English. Theresa was her name. Her father was an Ambassador to Mexico from England, and she her two siblings were raised in the mountains of Chiapas, in a very beautiful place. When her father retired, he stayed there for a time, and when the family finally moved back to England, this woman decided to remain in Mexico. She was quite a lady, an exquisite being." Twin Dreamers held her hands out, indicating that the woman was tall and slender.

"She would get material and make dresses, English-looking dresses. She came to live with our family because she, too, was a shaman. She had had abilities all of her life and could never understand them. She lived with us because we understood her and she understood us. She took a great liking to me and, to make a very long story short, she taught me how to speak English. That is why I have always been able to speak it well. She referred to her speech as 'the Queen's English.' In turn, I would teach her about dreaming. I remember one particular day very well. We were sitting by a river that ran through the jungle near our village. This river never went fast. It was always slow-moving water. It looked almost like glass." Twin Dreamers reached out her hands and put them on the sandy dirt where we were sitting, smoothing it. "The water was always so smooth," she said.

She cocked her head and looked at me, saying, "You know, we called it the 'River of Dreams,' and surely it helped one to dream as you lay in the sand beside it. Theresa and I used to lay side-by-side in the sand by this river, holding hands. As the river moved slowly by us, we would close our eyes and I would take her out of her body, into her dream body. We go out of our bodies every night that we sleep, everyone does, but we just don't realize it unless you know about dreaming. People don't realize we have a dream body and that you can move into other spaces, other areas, other dimensions where you can learn many wonderful things that you might not be able to learn here.

"So I would take her, and we would go to Europe, and she would explain things to me about England, about the beautiful cathedrals, and about different parts of the world. We traveled everywhere, Theresa and I. She was a great teacher. As English people would say, she was like a saint. She told me about Saint Theresa of Avilla and how she had created a monastery. She taught me things I would never have known about otherwise.

"My Theresa would look around the jungle and say, 'This is my monastery. This is my enjoyment. The jungle watches me and when I move, when I do things, I know that I change the way the jungle is looking at me. I know that as I watch the jungle and love the jungle, that it, too, loves me, and when I leave it is lonely without me, very lonely. And I am lonely for the jungle when I leave.'

"So I learned very early on that as you look at a mountain, the mountain enjoys you seeing it and it changes for you every day in the sunlight. It gives you a new gift by showing you a different face every time you look. It likes your relationship. When you leave that mountain, it misses your looking and you miss seeing it. Do you understand?"

"Yes," I said. "I do understand it so well."

"So," Twin Dreamers continued. "My life was a shaman life. I learned about good things and bad things, bad things being the things you don't use and good things being the things that are meant to help people, to heal people, through story, through experience. The reason that I climb up into trees and do silly things is because Theresa taught me to do them. Theresa and one of the men from the village who just loved to climb trees. This man would go up and get fruit and leaves out of the trees, sometimes eggs out of a nest. From an early age, I learned to climb trees and sit on the branches. We would go up in the trees and find a way to lean against the tree and listen to the birds. In a way, we would become the birds because the birds were looking at us and we were looking at the birds from our souls. All the people in the tribe would laugh; they thought it was great fun. Every once in a while, they would join us up in the trees, but for the most part, it was Theresa and I who did this. In the process, I learned to speak English very well.

"It wasn't until later on that Theresa, in her aging, had to leave the jungle and go home to her family in England. She said there was something she 'had to take care of.' She left and never returned, but we vowed to travel in our dreams to see each other, and we did. We became part of that extraordinary ability of being able to find people anywhere, and we did that until she passed on into another lifetime where she was needed more than this one. Before she passed away, she sent a courier with a great deal of money. Money was not something that our tribe needed in any sense of the word, but her money was used to create an irrevocable park out of the areas of the jungle where we were raised.

And it is still a park, today, and nobody can come in and cut those beautiful trees that we loved to climb in.

"You know," she said, jolting us both back to the present. "I'm sitting here watching myself talking to you. Me, an old broken-down Indian woman." She took a twig in her hand and cracked it into two pieces. "And you there, seemingly much younger and stronger than you would have been but for what you've learned. We have done well together, and we have much more to do. But I do see a few things about your world reflected back. It is about power and how we hold power. It is all held very close inside us like a holy wind within each of our lives. You have seen me, Black Wolf, change from a beautiful young woman into an old decrepit lady with no teeth."

She laughed and slapped her thighs, and I laughed with her. She could not laugh without making me laugh, no matter how serious our labors were at the moment.

"You see, it's a dream, but those are only words to people who don't understand the depth. Maybe we should talk about the dream."

"I've had a great deal of trouble teaching the dream," I said, "because people are under so much stress that it is hard for them to concentrate. They can't devote their time to getting out of their bodies and into the astral plane, let alone into higher dimensions. I have had great trouble with that, Twin Dreamers."

"I know," she said. "I have watched you and this situation. It is of concern to me because I can play in ways that you cannot. What good does my play do for someone who is working in New York in a nine-to-five job? How do we reach those people, you and I? We have all spent our lifetimes trying to reach people."

"But maybe that's not the answer," I said.

"What do you think it might be, then?" she asked.

"I think, perhaps, that it is like Agnes said to me when we were in the Himalayas. She said, 'You have one responsibility, and that is to enlighten yourself.' Maybe that's what I need to focus on: my own enlightenment. My enlightenment includes my school and all the people I love, all the people who have come to me, for whom I feel so very, very responsible. I feel like maybe I failed them. I can't get people out of their by-rote, ordinary lives when I seem to need to."

"But you see," Twin Dreamers said quickly, "that's the problem. You are trying. There is no trying. You either do it or you don't, and some things you simply cannot do. You cannot shift others for them. It is something they have to become willing to work for, themselves. You, Lynn, can only be what you are, that shining light that expresses your grace to others. They can feel it and they can see it, if they choose. The problem, of course, is that it is hard to acknowledge another's beauty when you cannot see that same beauty in yourself."

"But, Twin Dreamers, let's go back to the dream, the sacred dream."

"Yes," she said, looking at the stars. She began to draw a design in the dirt with a broken stick.

"What are you drawing?" I asked.

"I'm drawing the constellation of the Pleiades," she said. "Our wisdom originally came from the Pleiades, so they say. I know the Pleiades."

"Is that where you go at night," I asked, "when you seem so very far away in your dreams?"

"Yes, I go to the Pleiades. That is my home. I came from Panama in this lifetime, and maybe other places, but I come from the Pleiades. I can tell you a story, a story that I don't even ask you to believe. I will tell you a story of my choosing," she said.

She was getting further and further away from me. Her voice was changing, and there was an accent to her words, something I had not heard in many years.

"Do you remember a long time ago," she said, "when we were sitting in the north of Canada and we talked about a story? I told you about how a story stalks you. We had much fun. I told you there was a story wrapping itself around your consciousness, trying to get your attention. It was teasing you, as stories do.

"Yes, I think that is worthy of talking about," she said, "but I have had lifetimes that have stalked me, not just stories. They became inherent in all that I do. Shields have helped me understand life force as it flows from one lifetime to another."

She began making circles in the sand with designs of stars and lightning flashes.

"You need to learn to have steel inside you. That steel is what a lot of women don't understand. They try to pick up a male shield when they are out in the world, instead of holding a strong female shield," she said.

"What is the difference?" I asked her.

"The difference is that when you as a modern woman pick up a male shield, you drop your female power and your beauty, your ability to have extraordinary passion and intuition. It's not supposed to be this way. You are not supposed to drop your female shield, your ability for spontaneous creativity, for which women have an innate instinct. Don't try to become a male.

"In the female shield we learn that we respond differently, and this is most important. You see, there are times when we do have to fight, when we have to use all of the power and will at our disposal in order to survive. We want to think that we're in a civilized world where fighting doesn't have to happen, where we just need to be firm. Sometimes it takes more than that. The problem is that when a woman goes into a male shield, she picks up an energy that is not part of her. When you do that, you become someone you are not, someone who does not move or speak, think or respond with your own truth."

She twisted her hair through her fingers and once again began to move around in a circle.

"Then you allow yourself to move into a place of unprepared fear, which is what I call dropping your own true shield. When you have worked hard to strengthen your female shield so that you can move out into the world as the woman of power you are, you have a kind of steel within you that nobody else has. Not even a male warrior can have that kind of power.

"And that is something that your people need to learn. Your world needs the balance between the strong male shield and the strong female shield. You have to learn how to balance these energies in yourselves and in your world without dropping one or the other. When you drop one or the other shield, you lose the vision, the insight, the power that shield gives you.

"You have to learn what the male shield is all about and what the female shield is all about. The male shield teaches you to move out into the world in an organized and forceful way so that you can be effective in your endeavors. The female shield takes you into your intuition, teaching you to be receptive to the energy that is going on around you so that you will understand it and know how to move through it successfully, receptive to new ideas. As a woman, you have to know how to be organized and forceful in your actions if you want to get anything done. But you do not become a man. You do not move out of your receptivity. You do not separate yourself from the voice of wisdom and intuition within you that sees the truth of a situation, unclouded by emotional fear or mental judgment and criticism.

"I see your strong female shield in the world, Lynn, but I also see it lacking in you from time to time. I think it's hard for you to keep that steel when you feel the onslaught of the world, its opinions and its ignorance in areas where you can see so much possibility. When you see so much, when you see the over-all picture, it is very difficult. The trick for you is to learn how to pick up the male shield effectively but stand your ground as a woman, stand your ground knowing the truth of your dreams and your vision."

Circling Back: "Hero or House Pet, Which Are You?"

"We are born wild like a mountain lion, yet to live in civilization we become sheep at a very young age. We become tame. But we are not house pets. We are fierce and wild by nature. Movement between one life situation and another is essential. Movement, action, is the key that unlocks the door to understanding. Dream on this. Consider what is left of your instinctual nature."[2]

When I think of who are the heroes of my world, I think of these words of Twin Dreamers, a Kuna woman of Panama who is one of the most remarkable people I have ever known.

We live in a country where we have extraordinary personal freedom, by modern standards, yet everywhere we look, we see people absolutely hobbled by their own self-imposed limitations. We see a culture strangling on its own neediness.

Children, with their brilliant imaginations and unbounded curiosity, grow up being taught to speak when spoken to and believe what they are told even if their own senses tell them differently. Women are taught that to speak of our power as women is to be shunned by much of society.

---

2   From *Star Woman*. © 1986 by Lynn Andrews.

When you take the time to listen to our societies, so often you hear a strangled sound. It is the sound of people who are afraid to speak their own truth, who don't even know, perhaps, what their own personal truth is. Jesus, Buddha, Michelangelo, even Thomas Jefferson, with his devotion to the rights of all people, would have a very difficult time being accepted in our world today.

It's not that this is anything new. People with special vision have always seen more than those around them, and they are often not well accepted because of it. The shaman, the healer, the artist, the thinker, all see with new eyes in a world that believes it is held together by uniformity. Early thinkers who believed that the earth was round were burned at the stake. Albert Einstein's teachers described him as mentally slow, lost in his own foolish dreams. Louisa May Alcott's family urged her to give up her dreams of becoming a writer and be a seamstress or servant, instead. Beethoven, who preferred to compose his own music over studying the techniques of others, was told by one of his teachers that he would never make it as a composer.

It is always difficult to be an individual. It is risky sticking your neck out, poking your head above the crowd to express new ideas. It is even risky to listen to new ideas with an open heart and mind. But for me, to be fully alive is to risk all that we know for the great adventure of the unknown, filled as it is with infinite possibility, the sacred mystery that calls to us from the depths of our being.

Nobody owns the truth. Why are we so quick to give our truth away when someone disagrees with us or doesn't give us the encouragement that we expected? If you believe in your dreams, isn't it worth taking the risk of bringing them to life? Your life is worth the risk. Living your truth is your heritage. It is your birthright, a right that is not available to all people across this world.

To me, living your own personal truth is what makes a hero. Greatness often lies not just in our achievements but in the obstacles we overcome to get there, the number of times we pick ourselves up off the ground when something doesn't work out, look at what went wrong and start all over again. As Winston Churchill once said, "Success is going from failure to failure without losing your enthusiasm!"

History gives us ample examples of people who do just that. Abraham Lincoln was defeated at the ballot box many times and he even failed at business before being elected President of the United States. Walt Disney was fired from a newspaper for not having good ideas. He, along with Henry Ford and a host of America's most successful business leaders, went through numerous bankruptcies before they finally got it right. NASA failed over a dozen times before finally launching a rocket into outer space, and they had to fight for their existence after each and every failure.

When the world pushes you, and it pushes everyone, make no mistake about that, you have to take the risk of pushing back. A person of power attains her goal only by remaining whole as a person, not giving away her own personal truth, not quitting when things get difficult.

Your life has meaning. Your life is special. Your life is like no other. So celebrate the integrity of your own very special personality. Follow your truth and don't be afraid to fail or succeed. If something doesn't work out the way you want it to, stick with it until you find out what went wrong, and then do what you have to do to change it. Michael Jordan was cut from his high school basketball team, but that didn't stop him!

Always remember this: no matter what you do, the Great Spirit has a hand on your back, breathing the power of truth through the wind. So when you are struggling, remember to breathe. Feel the wind, the breath of the Great Spirit at your back. Breathe in deeply and draw strength, for you are taking in the breath of God.

When you consciously breathe with the Great Spirit, you are never separate and you are never alone. This is one of our greatest stumbling blocks in life, our fear of being alone, our fear of being separate, of being different, of being looked at as a failure if something doesn't work out the first time we try it. These fears are the main reasons we give our truth away and quit on our dreams, and we die a little bit every time we do.

It is when you heal the fear of being different, with an open heart, that you begin to see what your life is really about. It is about the search for meaning, finding the meaning that is true for you and then acting on it.

To me, the true meaning of greatness is feeling the presence of great truth and taking it in as the inspiration from spirit that it is, and then manifesting that inspiration into the world. When you look at the people in your world who stand out as heroes to you, what is it about them that makes them so heroic? Is it not their ability to inspire you to be more than you ever thought you could be?

Our thoughts are but forms of energy. What you think, you become. So watch what you think and celebrate your own truth in everything that you do. Become a hero to yourself, and your world will always be filled with heroes.

9

AMINA

A COOL BREEZE SWEPT OVER the Red Sea. Whitecaps formed and I imagined a moment without unforgiving heat. Jagged mountains rose up in forbidding daggers of granite towards the relentless sun.

A seeming fortress of rock surrounds both the road and St. Catherine's Monastery at the foot of Mount Sinai. No wonder Moses found himself in this valley to climb to the voice of God. The Sinai is the most desolate, challenging landscape I have seen.

Yet Amina, small and slight of stature, holds this rugged landscape within her soul. In her full, colorful skirt with bangles and red fringe, she walked towards me, down the path barren and secure from others' eyes. Her white blouse was full and feminine, and covered with bright necklaces of silver, gold, and lapis lazuli. Her long gray hair was loosely tied back with combs that had tiny dangles catching the light.

"You're Bedouin, Amina!" I cried. She was a far cry from the grim, *burqa*-clad women I had been seeing all over Cairo.

She held out her hand to me, tears brimming behind her eyelids. In the palm of her hand, a silver shield reflected the light, but actually the shield itself seemed permeated by an awesome glow.

"For you. It will protect you always," she said. For a moment, a ray of sun reflected into my eyes, obscuring my vision, and then it was gone. I put my arms around her and thanked her, then she hung the shield on a necklace around my neck. Amina is a member of the Sisterhood of the Shields, and I was meeting her in the land of her birth for the first time.

I slipped a turquoise and coral ring onto her finger and said, "It was made for me by Charles Lollama, a Hopi Snake Priest, and old friend."

"It is beautiful," Amina said, as she touched it to her heart. "We have much to talk about," she said, pulling me down the slippery path.

We turned an abrupt corner and walked into a shadowy crevice. If someone had been looking, we would have completely disappeared from view. Tall granite walls surrounded us.

Amina lit a torch and we picked our way through a labyrinthine tunnel. We came to limestone that had white mica reflecting the flame. Standing before the entrance to a tomb-like room was a statue of Sekhmet, the lion-headed goddess of war who is one of the oldest Egyptian deities, whose name means "The Powerful One."

Inside the room, golden images lined the walls from floor to a high, vaulted ceiling. In one corner was a stone sarcophagus. I was not familiar with this transformational chamber, and it didn't appear to be open to the public. Beautiful silk scarves in white and gold had been draped over the stone and many candles were burning in handcrafted alabaster containers.

Amina and I sat on the floor. She asked me to close my eyes as she picked up a lavender silk scarf and placed it over my head. Then she began singing in her own language, playing the rhythm on a small hand-painted drum. Her song echoed strangely and was hypnotic.

The air was cool in my lungs, sedating and pure. I closed my eyes and immediately I began to see geometric designs and holograms.

"Time will dance for all of you who understand the Hermetic Holograms. 'As above, so below.'" Your scientists, the quantum physicists, the great thinkers of the world are proving these 5,000-year-old teachings to be true." I saw pyramids on squares in circles. "It is simple: it takes absolute intent from your open heart. Feel not the rain, but seek the serenity of love. Love truly is the healing element of our world. Allow yourself to dream now of a life of learning, wisdom, and reflection."

As I listened to Amina singing, I floated into a valley, green and surrounded by rolling hills and trees. I imagined a different time, the times before sand, when we celebrated our uniqueness and our glorious differences rather than killed over them. We shared ideas in books and great halls filled with learning. We loved and we found an ultimate peace.

I felt an overwhelming love, not dependent on an object or thought. I was imbedded in bliss, and bliss was imbedded in me. Soon I was lifting myself out of consciousness and putting on my scarf. I lay down at the feet of Sekhmet, a beautiful glimmering stone carving. I began to drift on into a state of deep dreaming.

I could see the lotus incense surrounding me and I breathed of it deeply. I traveled through the waves of alabaster color and went deeper and deeper into the desert, a different part of the desert from the Sinai valley. I felt surreal and singular against stone twisted towers where Moses had walked millenniums ago.

Then shifting, I saw up ahead, through a strangely formed mist, the height of the Great Pyramid of Giza. I was familiar with this area; it had been one of the first places I had ever gone in Egypt and I felt excited in the dream. I floated now on some sort of energy pillow. I wasn't sure that the pillow was being created by me. I had a sense that I was being carried by something other than my own life force. I realized I was asleep. I kept thinking I should waken and yet I could not. There was something that kept me from leaving the dream.

The mist settled around me again and suddenly I was at the top of the Giza Pyramid, high in the air above the stark desert of shifting sands. I was standing, now, on the top of the pyramid and there were a couple of small carved stone rooms that I had never seen before. Perhaps they had been there in ancient times.

Behind me, from what I could see, were people. A small fire was burning in each small room, ceremonial lotus smoke thick in the air, dancing shadows on the ancient walls. The moon was coming up over the horizon. It was beautiful, hauntingly bright. I was aware of a gentle sway of Sekhmet, which brought me back for just a moment from my dreaming. The scent of lotus was strong and then there was another scent, as well, sweet, very sweet, almost like the scent of honey.

Again I was whisked away by some unseen force into another world, and I suddenly felt the sense of air rushing by me, as if I were flying. I realized, then, that I was flying through space, that there was a momentum to my consciousness that could not be denied. I flew somewhere out in space, out into the universe or inside into my own inner universe. I felt the brushing of wings fluttering from somewhere. I felt as if I was being turned over and over and over again in an unusual fashion. The turning generated a warmth.

Then, suddenly, out of nowhere came a vision, a picture of different aspects of my life. Once again, I was seeing pictures from a long, long time ago and these were happy pictures, not pictures of pain but of joy . . . pictures of when I got my first pony, my first puppy; when I found my own way home from school in kindergarten, walking all by myself. There was the joy of spring scent as hundreds of pictures fluttered by in a montage of light and darkness. I knew absolutely that all we experience has been written.

Ahead of me, I saw great beings of light—women and men of high degree, I assumed. My soul in the shape of a round shield sat before them on a long table, and they were studying it. As I approached, this shield which was my spirit shield began to spin and create a great shining that resonated with my inner world and my shaman center. It was as if I had taken my hand away from over my eyes and had seen reality and my position in it for the very first time.

I have always been here, I thought.

But I hadn't realized so many aspects of life. Therefore, I became a wanderer of spirit, trekking through the mists that seduce me into the mystery, the cloud moving winds at my back. Perhaps this was a luxury I could no longer afford. I had learned much and now was the time to give back these precious gifts.

The Great Beings, God Beings, smiled and nodded in appreciation as I drifted away, back into my dream of Amina and the physical world. After a short time, I tried to sit up on the floor, floundering and waving my arms, and I fell back onto the ground, losing my balance as I stared at Sekhmet. I was positive that she had shoved me with her great paw. But Sekhmet was an inanimate statue. I was awake.

Amina and I laughed as she gave me a hand. We both understood the power of Sekhmet. It was early morning and the sun was just rising as we left the sacred cave in a ceremonial way. Two small, white camels awaited us. Amina was a deeply loved sister.

"I will study the holograms. I've held them in my mind. *Shokrun.* Thank you, Amina, dear one." I held my hand over my heart. We mounted the camels and disappeared in opposite directions as the early dawn light began to terrace the rocky valley in a pink golden light.

Circling Back: "Shaman Woman in Egypt"

In the beginning there is love, the pure, unconditional love of the Great Spirit and all the beings of light in the universe. Then we come into this earth walk and lose our way. We become distracted by the frailties of physical existence. We forget about the over-arching embrace of Divine love and the great mysteries of life from which we are born. Sometimes we have to come back for many lifetimes of forgetting and remembering before we finally find our way back home to Divine love.

From the time we landed at Cairo Airport and I first set foot on Egyptian soil, I felt a personal transformation of homecoming, perhaps for the first time in my life. I had not visited this prodigious land in this lifetime, except in dreams, had not laid my eyes on the great pyramids nor walked through the temples of the gods. I had yet to journey through the sands of antiquity to the banks of the River Nile, animating force of this sacred world.

Yet there was something about this compassionate and dangerous land that drew me to its breast. It seemed to whisper, *"You can breathe, now, for you have come home."* It brought tears to my eyes. From that point on, Egypt became the discovery of remarkable windows of perception, riding at dawn around the pyramids on magnificent Arabian horses and camels as the mists rose from the sand and the city of Cairo, the relentless sun coming down from the heavens and showing us our way on this pilgrimage to the gods.

The alchemy of life is about transformation, about nurturing the lead of your everyday existence into the gold of inner balance and the mystical harmony of your spiritual and physical being.

Somehow, in Egypt, you drop belief structures. You surrender the fences you have put around your consciousness. You realize that you do not need them; they only limit you.

You feel in a way that you are in the mind of God, whoever your Gods or Goddesses are, as you experience the frequency, the vibration of your heartfelt connection with the goddess Isis, Mother of Love; with Akhenaton, the unexpected ruler of the Middle Kingdom who never intended to be pharaoh, whose legacy as the first pharaoh and one of the earliest leaders to talk about a single god is still reverberating across our world today. You are in the mind of God along with the pharaohs and the workers of the temples.

Ancient Egyptian temples were not just places of worship. They were places of work, places of celebration for the people and their gods and goddesses. The ancient Egyptians didn't simply sit before their gods and goddesses in adulation and adornment; they interacted with them. They didn't inveigle their gods to do for them nearly so much as they did for their gods, and this is reflected in all of the paintings and carvings on every wall, ceiling, balustrade of their temples. As individuals and as a people, they devoted much of their conscious living to nurturing their relationship with the gods and honoring them with a creative ingenuity, an artistry, and an engineering skill that is astounding. It was part of their conscious awareness of life.

When you interact with the gods and goddess of your existence, understanding that they are within you and a part of you, informing your life, just as you are within and a part of them, you begin to reclaim lost or missing aspects of yourself.

In Egypt, there is even a remembering of Hermes, the Greek god of eloquence who served as messenger of the gods. It is as if he is heralding the original teachings of Ancient Egypt, just for you. You don't remember the words, perhaps, but you remember the sense of vibration. When I was in the Kings' Chamber in the Pyramid of Giza, I saw orbs of light flying around the room, beautiful symbols of history that were visiting us, watching us, and joining us in ceremony with the sarcophagus and the healing ceremonies of forgetting and remembering.

You can never really teach anyone about power and the magic of transformation with words. You must use experience. You can look into the eyes of a woman of power and see that she has years of truth ahead of you. If you open your heart, her eyes can quicken you like a river heading toward the rapids.

In Egypt, you can take a boat ride to the Temple of Philae, the delicate, elegant, quintessentially feminine temple of the Goddess Isis, and be quickened. This graceful antiquity was built over 2500 years ago on the rocky island of Philae, in the middle of the Nile River, to honor a Goddess that had first been written about nearly 2500 years before.

The entire island of Philae, including its ancient temples, was submerged by the building of the first Aswan Dam in 1906. In the 1970's, over a nine-year period of time, the United Nations Educational, Scientific and Cultural Organization came together with a community of nations to dismantle and move the Temple of Philae, meticulously, stone-by-numbered-stone, from its ancient home on Philae and reconstruct it on the much higher Egilica Island, where it now stands. What an alchemist you are, Goddess Isis, Mother of Love, that even in our jaded and embattled modern world, whole nations can be inspired to rise above their self-imposed ideologies of separation and domination to come together and gift this magnificent Temple back to you and to all the people of this world.

As you reflect upon the remarkable ingenuity and workmanship of the ancient Egyptians in creating this marvelous temple *in the middle of a river* and the massive effort that it took us in our time to dismantle, move and reconstruct it in its original form *in a different part of the river,* you cannot help but realize that you are in the presence of one of the greatest animating forces in the entire universe. That presence is love, and the force is the power of pure, unconditional love to transform anything and everything in life, including ourselves and our world.

So often today, our embrace of love is wrapped tightly around the experience of sexuality, as if that is the be all and end-all of relationship. I see love as a ladder, with sexuality, the attraction that compels you into a relationship whether it is with another person or with some fabulous masterpiece you yearn to create, as the bottom rung. This attraction is what wakes you up. It enlivens your spirit, gets your creative juices flowing. It is but the beginning of the great power of love.

When I speak of power, I am not talking about control over someone or something in terms of manipulation and domination. I am speaking of power as the energy that flows between all things and, specifically, I am speaking of power as the understanding of the spiritual energy that flows through all beings. In the shaman's world view, this is the essence of power in its truest form: the spiritual energy that flows through all beings. The first lesson of power is that we are all alone. The final lesson of power is that we are all one. We are all one with the Great Spirit, even the rocks and the trees, the plants, the animals, all things of this world. We are all part of one another.

If you want to understand the timelessness of your existence, sit with a rock and meditate; go into its slow, steady vibration. That rock has perhaps been part of this earth for millions of years. It has witnessed things that our minds cannot even begin to fathom, and it will share the essence of these mysteries with you if you will open yourself to the oneness, instead of being closed off by your separation from that rock. In the Great Spirit, there is no separation, and thus is true power born, for when there is no separation there is wholeness. Life is complete. Its power is not diluted and drained away.

As you stand with the Goddess Isis in the Temple of Philae with all its remarkable history, you realize that love and power are mates. You remember that love is the essence of your life's blood. Without love, the soul cannot exist. Controlling others is not true power. Laying your reality over someone else's is actually the antithesis of power.

When you fall in love, be it with a person or an idea or a dream, you are making a bid for the power of love to come to you. Know this: when you make a bid for power, power will test you. If you turn the power of your attraction into a mechanism for domination and control, you fail the test of power. You fail, because in seeking to control, you destroy the energy that flows between you and that which you strive to love. Without that energy, you will eventually fall into the abyss of loneliness and emptiness; power will defeat you, and then it will leave you. You will have no true intimacy with life, nothing to spark the great dance of passion and creativity, which are the offspring of power and love. Power without love leaves you without any sustaining energy to keep the feeling of power alive. The true test of power is the ability to hold strength with open hands, and that only happens when you let your passion and creativity propel you up the ladder of love instead of remaining stuck on the bottom rung of life.

The middle rung of the ladder, then, is creativity, the creativity that is awakened through your passion, through the energies of love-making. What is 'love-making' really but nurturing something or someone you care about deeply to their fullest creative potential? Passion and creativity are partners. They inspire, inform and invigorate one another. Without each other, there is a huge imbalance in energy that will ultimately lead to the collapse of what you are trying to do. Can you see how the control that we all so desperately seek in today's world is actually irrelevant? It is a great saboteur of life.

The highest rung on the ladder of love is always your fire, your connection with the Divine, with the Great Spirit. This is what gives birth to compassion, which is one of the highest expressions of love. Compassion is a natural aspect of spirit that is spontaneous and unassuming. It is being attuned to other beings in the world, not just people but to the whole of your environment. It is an expression of your oneness with life. When the creativity of sexual energy brings you into spiritual contact with your Divine force, then love arises and transforms the passion of your attraction into compassion and divine inspiration. You become one with what it is you are trying to manifest into the world, and in that oneness is where you find your power.

Such is the power of the Goddess Isis in her great Temple at Philae that she helps you remember the alchemy of life, awakening you to truths that you already carry within your being, waiting for you to become aware. You don't have to go to Egypt and walk through her Temple to be quickened by the power of love, for love is everywhere, in all things. All you need do is surrender the fences you have put around your consciousness and become open to the natural flow of life. Let go of your need to control. Open yourself, instead, to the great power of love.

Welcome passion and creativity into your hut and make them your partners, and be amazed as you awaken the abilities and the brilliance that already reside within you. Then, when you can, come to Egypt and share your joy and your bliss with Isis. There is a very good reason why the ancient Egyptians revered her so and went to such lengths to acknowledge her presence in their lives. Just look at what she inspires humanity to accomplish.

10

AN ANCIENT AND MODERN PROPHECY

ONE AFTERNOON IN CAIRO, I got a phone call from the front desk of the Mena House telling me that there was a woman saying she was an old friend of mine who wanted to meet me in the bar, and could I please come down? I was intrigued.

I was wearing a white scarf with sequins and beads on the very thin cotton, wrapped around my shoulders over a simple black dress. I let a friend in the hotel know where I was going simply because I had no idea who I was meeting. A shiver of excitement skittered through me as I went down in the elevator, looking at old tin-type photographs of turn-of-the-century parties, horses pulling carriages up to the Mena House Oberoi and the palace, which were on the walls. In these pictures, there was nothing between the Mena House and the pyramids, and it was an exquisite image. A photograph of camels and horses caught my eye. The animals were standing, looking at the people, wondering what they were doing there, how they could possibly be feeling? *What a beautiful time to have been in Egypt*, I thought, *before all the 20th century wars.*

By then, I was in the lobby and walking across the crowded entryway with tourists from all over the world, speaking different languages, and into the bar. It was cool, darkly lit with candles and oil pots of lotus. A subtle, clean fresh scent filled the air. I looked around the bar and saw a few couples sitting at various tables. Then I saw a woman sitting at a table in the corner and I knew intuitively that this was the person I was supposed to meet.

She stood up when she saw me. I did not know her, I didn't think. She had a lovely cream colored suit on, made of what looked like silk that was fitted to her slender form, high heels, beautiful dark hair pulled back in a bun at the nape of her neck. She was startlingly beautiful, with high cheekbones and beautifully tanned skin. She wore full makeup and an exquisite necklace of lapis lazuli and gold. She was elegant. She could have been a prime minister's wife.

I walked slowly toward her, wondering who in the world she was? Then, with stunned surprise, I realized that this beautiful woman, elegant beyond imagination, was Amina, the woman of the Sisterhood of the Shields whom I had met outside St. Catherine's Monastery in the Sinai Desert, at the foot of Mt. Sinai. When I met her, she had appeared to be a beautiful Bedouin woman, wholly different from this sophisticated, elegant person standing in front of me.

I reached out my arms and gave her a hug in absolute awe and disbelief. She laughed at my stunned surprise, said nothing except, "Please join me," in perfectly accented English. She took my hands and we stared into each other's eyes. I wondered what it was that I was here to see? A conversation I had many years ago with Carlos Castaneda flashed through my mind, when he told me about a meeting he had in Mexico City with a *nagual* woman, a woman of the highest degree of dreaming and power. She had always met Carlos as a traditional *curandera*. On one occasion, however, she appeared transformed into a sophisticated aristocrat. As I sat there listening to Amina, this memory and imagining flitted into my mind and then faded away.

Amina spoke to me of a prophecy about the state of Egypt and what was to happen in the not too distant future. She told me of a revolution that was about to occur, and she said that it was to be a very dangerous time for the whole world, that I needed to pay attention to what she was saying to me. She talked to me about Hosni Mubarak, then president of Egypt, who was a dictator and a very hard man, who ruled this disparate country with an iron fist. She told me that there was great poverty in the country, that the young people who were coming up in the villages, all under the age of thirty, were very restless. She said they had no jobs, no way to support their families. She said that it was a very frightening time for them, they were angry that there was such wealth in their world and yet such poverty and pain, as well.

She said a revolution was coming that has been a long time fomenting, that age-old clashes between the Coptic Christians and the Sunni Muslims of Egypt were going to get drastically worse, and that in the background are many terrorist factions, waiting for opportunity to show itself to them.

She said it has been written in Bedouin prophecy for a very long time that these factions will try to take over the entire Middle East and the world as we know it.

I said, "But Amina, how can I possibly do anything? I am so unfamiliar with the politics of this country. I have only met people who are involved with its history, the museums and antiquities."

I ran my hands over the beautiful tabletop. A waiter came by and asked if we wanted anything, and I ordered a Diet Coke as Amina ordered Ginger Ale. The waiter, a tall Egyptian man, looked at her and nodded his head almost imperceptibly, then walked away with our order.

I looked at her and smiled, "You know him."

"Yes," she said. "He comes from a village near mine in the southern part of Egypt, the lower part of Egypt. I don't know that I will be able to see you again."

"Why Amina?" I asked, alarmed. "There is so much I want to learn from you."

She said, "There are hard times coming and no one can know who I am or what I do. It would mean my instant death." She held the scarf that she was wearing up, around her head, for a moment, as if shielding from the wind or the sun, and looked at me with the most infinite gaze. Her dark eyes, pools of intensity, very alive and almost liquid, watched me react to what she was saying. I felt that I needed to do something, but what could I do?

"The important thing," she continued, "is that you know and that you teach your people that we are all like grains of sand going through an hourglass. All people who are alive at this time, the whole of humanity across this earth, are at the neck of the hourglass." She paused, holding up a fist. "We are being squeezed through the hourglass, and the stress and the impact are so intense that we do not know how to deal with this new input of energy.

"I use the word 'energy' but in fact it is the life force from our Creator Gods and it has happened before in our history, many thousands of years ago. It was not treated well at that time, and we cannot repeat old mistakes. The 'One Who Knew' at that time worshiped the sun, but it was not the sun that he elevated. He elevated the power of light." She swung her fingers around and continued, "You know about the light."

I thought I could see flecks, sparks of light, coming from the ends of her fingers in the near darkness of the bar. The candle flickered on the table and flared up for a moment, and went back down. I was startled and sat back.

She said, "Yes, it is the light that is infusing us with power."

"But light is always defined by the darkness," I said. "That's how we see the beauty of the light, isn't that so, Amina?"

She said, "Yes, it is true. And because of the light, because we have a new ability to see the truth of things, there will be darkness like we've never known. And it will mean we evolve or our existence as human beings will be gone.

She flattened her hand out in front of her, her palms just above the table, beautiful hands, fingernails lacquered with polish, her beautiful wedding ring, a diamond, courageous for her to wear, I believed, because it was so large.

"Amina, where do you come from? Who are you? You're obviously not a woman from a village in southern Egypt, along the Nile."

She responded, "Yes, my people are and we are ancient people here."

I said, "I know, it's a kindness. I understand the poverty and the pain. I don't understand the anger. The images of anger we are shown are of people who have never experienced the poverty. Instead, they are plying it, trading on it like it is a commodity. How do we solve this?" I asked.

She told me that the light was coming.

"What do you mean, 'The light is coming?'"

And she said, "He Who Carries It."

And I said, "He?"

A messiah?

She laughed, giggling as she had when I first met her in the Sinai. And I wondered for a moment at how light her skin was. Even though the Bedouin are said to be Caucasian, from the north, they are almost black in color, with well defined features. They have spent ages in the sun and they are tanned deeply. It dawned on me that, of course, this is the element that had surprised me when I first saw Amina this morning. I had previously watched her on the side of a mountain of shale and granite, with the extremely severe sunlight glinting off her colors, her bangles and her hair blowing in the wind. I had wondered at the time at the lightness of her skin. Just being in the sun for a week, you would expect someone to be sunburned or dark.

I think she was following my thoughts, because she said, "You know, Lynn. I flow with the wind and the powers of the world, like the sand flows in the tsunami and the wind storms across the desert. It covers everything. And I dig out of that sand after the storms and I rise again on my horse. I ride my beautiful stallion across the dunes. He is grey and white. He is beautiful; he is like a horse that you once rode."

She looked at me intensely. I thought, *What?* I thought of my horses. Then I thought of Arion and asked, "You mean Arion?"

"Yes," she answered. "You wrote of him in *Star Woman*."

And I said, "How could that be?"

"He was your horse. I sent him to you to help you all those many years ago, and now you come to me and I have so little time. I so wish things were different." Gently she put her scarf over my head. "Through the horse's dreams, we will see each other." I fell silent and was simply flabbergasted.

She continued, "We are on different continents, in different mountains, in different deserts, and we are washed by the sea in different realms. But you must remember that we are as one. And if you exist here, in Cairo, in an ancient palace called the Mena House, you may have been here once before. You may have lived here. You may have experienced the pyramids long before this recorded time. You know of what I speak, the green alfalfa that grows by the Nile, so deeply rich with life force, before the dams were built, before Aswan, when the beauty of this country was led by the pharaohs and the great ones before them, many thousands of years ago. You remember in your blood."

She reached out her hands. I didn't know what to say. I looked at her with such happiness in my heart. She was kind, and yet there was a fierceness in her eyes that I thought I could learn about, that perhaps I needed in my life and have had trouble finding.

This was some years ago. As I look today, in 2011, at what I recorded during that time with Amina, I listen to the news that the Coptic Christians and the Muslims are clashing in fierce battles following the fall of the Mubarak government. Revolution now spreads across the desert like the relentless sun, hard, driving.

"This has happened before," Amina had said, *"and it was not well handled then. You can help your people to understand history, study it so we can change into a higher consciousness."*

Two dark-suited men entered the bar. They stood at each end and nodded to Amina. She stood up. As she placed a hand on mine, she said, "I need to go now, Little Wolf. See you soon." Momentarily, the two guards followed her out. She was gone. I sat at the table for some time as I realized the extreme danger she was in.

Circling Back: "World News, A Shaman's Point of View"

It is vital for us to be informed about what is happening in our world. How else are we going to know what needs to be healed on an earth that is in greater peril today than any previous time in human history, or how to heal it?

Yet every time I talk about the importance of paying attention to the news and world affairs, people say to me, "Lynn, why on earth do you want us to watch to the news? All it does is sensationalize everything bad, and I just can't stand it."

It is true that much of the evening news and front-page headlines dramatizes the flashiest events of our times, many of which are not really all that important, in ways that keep us riveted to our seats for the sake of ratings without truly informing us of anything.

At the same time, it is important to know what is happening down the block, around the corner or on the other side of the earth. We do not live in isolation anywhere in the world. What people do in a faraway land can have as much impact on our lives as what we, ourselves, do and do not do. Global warming and poverty impact every corner of this earth. Their causes come from everywhere, and it is going to take the combined efforts of every single one of us to heal them.

Over 2500 years ago, a very erudite hero of the Western world said, *"The only true crime is the crime of ignorance."* His name was Socrates and his words are as relevant to our world today as they were when he spoke them, probably more so now, given that today we possess a technology so fearsome that we are capable of wiping out entire cities in the blink of an eye. We need to know what we are doing before we do it. How else are we going to stop ourselves from repeating old catastrophes and creating new ones because of the stupidity of our own ignorance?

There is a great chasm between keeping yourself informed and merely watching the evening news or reading the front page. In this chasm lies all of the power that you can ever need to heal your life and heal our world from the news that we find so distressing.

That power is called *knowledge*, the knowledge that we gain by studying the events of our day and learning as much as we can about what is really behind them.

Knowledge is the first step towards wisdom, which is found in the balance between universal knowledge and the sanctuary of knowledge that is learned through our harmony and our struggles on Mother Earth. In wisdom, there is no fear. So if something impacts you so greatly as to ignite your fear or your anger, then make it important enough to learn about. Find out about it from as many different perspectives as you can.

Yes, we are living in a world that is fraught with chaos and confusion. It has been written about and prophesied for millenniums.

Yes, we are living in a world where negativity is too often the prevailing influence on human affairs.

But you do not have to be controlled by that negativity or chaos. We are well into the energy of "2012," going through the Crossing Times. The women of the Sisterhood of the Shields all say as one voice that this has happened before. It has happened before, and it will happen again. What we do about it in our time will determine whether we, as one people, will fail or succeed. They all say that great mistakes were made in the past. With as much knowledge as there is in the world today about what those mistakes were, there is no excuse for our repeating them.

And the women of the Sisterhood agree with us completely that this is not an easy time to be alive. These crossing times hurt us; they pain us. They are a struggle, and they challenge us to the core of our being.

But if we let them, these times teach us to have faith. As grim as it can be, the world news can teach us so much once we stop reacting to it and begin to learn from it. History is not the events of times gone by. History is what happens to us every day of our lives. It is also the story of what is to come as it grows out of the story of where we have been and what we do about it today.

These times teach us to pay attention and reach for the power of good in this world. We are literally mutating into a higher level of consciousness.

If we do not honor the dark side, then we will be ruled by the dark side. Always remember that if you become what you are trying to defeat, then what you are trying to defeat wins. When something negative affects you powerfully, you must look at it and understand it, and then turn your face away and let the light be your guide. To understand the darkness does not mean you become it. It means you examine it carefully, learning what it is made of, understanding its power and its limitations. Only then can you really do something to change it.

Great harm has been done on this earth by people who think they have all the answers. When you look at the dark side, it is important that you look at it from *all* sides, including the sides which seem to be diametrically opposed to what you believe are your best interests. If you do not see all sides of a thing, you will never discover its truth. If you do not discover its truth, how are you ever going to affect meaningful change?

There is also great good to be found in the daily news, for it alerts us to people and events that we might never have heard of otherwise. We can then go out and learn about what is good and right in our world in ways that enrich our lives beyond measure, bring us closer together as a people, all across the globe.

The Nobel awards, one of the highest honors in the entire world, are given out annually to people in six different disciplines who have made distinguished contributions in the interests of humanity, as they have been every December for over a century, since 1901. Did you know that the Nobel awards were initiated by a man named Alfred Nobel, a Swedish scientist and inventor who grew disillusioned by the potential for harm that could be caused by *his family's business* of making nitroglycerine and dynamite?

It is so often the really bad news that inspires us to achieve the highest good.

Did you know that the youngest Nobel laureate was 25 years old (for physics) and the oldest, 90 (economics)? That Swedish schoolteacher and Nobel laureate Selma Lagerlöf wrote a children's book about a naughty boy who became a goose that has inspired subsequent Nobel laureates in medicine as well as literature? That only 35 of the 809 Nobel laureates have been women? If you are a woman, does this knowledge inspire you to want to do something to change that? You can choose to become angry and live in the negativity of that statistic, or you can choose to go out and become the next woman Nobel laureate.

Always remember this: It takes only one person to plant the seeds of change. You have as much power to study and learn and work towards meaningful change as anyone else in the world. We can look at everything that is going on in the world today as negative, but it really is about taking away the roadblocks to a new consciousness that is ready to be born into this world.

There is nothing that stands in our way but ourselves.

11

AGNES WHISTLING ELK
Elkhorn Mountain, Revisited

I WAS DREAMING. Agnes and I were walking at the top of Elkhorn Mountain. In my dream, she had told me to feast and then fast so that we could celebrate "honoring my inward sun," as she called it, and she was once again saying to me, "It's good that you have held council with your ancestor father within you. The lights around your heart have been brightened and have found a good home."

Wait a minute, I thought through the dream. *I've been here before. I've even written about it.* It can be a startling experience to have your conscious thoughts interrupt a dream without waking up all the way. *The dream within the dream,* I realized. Part of me was trying to wake up and understand what was going on while another part of me was pulling me even deeper into the dream, where I was back on Elkhorn Mountain with Agnes, just as I had physically been with her on Elkhorn Mountain so many years ago. She had been giving me instruction on creating ghost dolls, and specifically a Mourner Doll and a Bone-Keeper Doll.

She had told me, "A mourner doll is you. It contains within its belly all your pain, greed, sorrow, and fears. In other words, it is a doll built and divined as a tangible expression of your intangible addictions. It is made of your crazy winds, your negativity, the impulses that have crippled your spirit. A mourner doll is your death." The bone-keeper doll, she had said, represented my life, the spirit that lives in my bones. "It holds your good intentions, the things that you want to accomplish in this lifetime, your spiritual and earth-plane goals."

I had made both dolls and when they were finished, Agnes and Ruby had built a ceremonial fire for me. "You will feel more balanced," Agnes had said.

Now Agnes and I were once again climbing down to the river at the bottom of Elkhorn Mountain and walking along its meandering banks. I realized through my dream, somehow, that this time I was noticing different aspects of the landscape than I had focused on before.

Agnes began to talk to me about my father. He was an enormous influence in my life. I was an only child and he treasured me, but to a fault. He would bring me too close, saying things like, "I wish I could find a wife just like you, who has your understanding."

I was six years old. I didn't want to be a wife. I needed a father, and I wanted to be a child. Somehow my relationship with him had robbed me of my childhood. I tried to be an adult. I tried to be grown up in all circumstances.

There were also frequent times that he would go into a rage about something, and I would end up being punished by him. It was a "push me, pull me" kind of situation. He was not an alcoholic, which is so often the cause of this erratic behavior. He had been born to an extraordinary family. His own father was a celebrated surgeon in Austria and Scandinavia and part of the Nobel family. I think that there had been expectations put on him that he could never meet or didn't even want to meet. I never understood it, because he was so brilliant and he taught me so much about books, papers, beauty, and about a woman taking her power. Yet, as he was giving me power, he was taking it away.

As Agnes and I walked along the river bank, I picked up feathers and little twisted sticks that looked like they had been part of the choke cherry bushes. Before, Agnes had told me to pick up things that "caught my eye." These twisted sticks were the things that caught my eye this time. Finally, Agnes pointed to a sandy beach and we sat down. She took all of the objects that we had gathered and placed them between us as if she was placing sacred things, like a prayer stick or a sacred pipe. She took great care.

"Tell me what you remember of your feelings when you think of your father," I remembered Agnes telling me before. It had been extremely uncomfortable for me to talk about my father with her then. I could still feel as I had at the time, like a clock being wound too tightly, rubber bands being pulled and snapping with the tension. Agnes noticed my distress and reached over, took hold of my shoulders and shook them back and forth.

"For heaven's sake, Little Wolf, loosen up," she said. "Your whole body is trailing after your emotions." I tried to sit up better. "You know, Little Wolf, your feelings, your emotions can deform you. It is not the path of heart to allow this into your life. It is not free and it is not good for you. You must make your self lodge bright and make your *heava* sit up and take notice." I remembered her saying those same words the last time we were at Elkhorn Mountain. *Heava,* the spirits of place and your own personal power. I remembered her saying, "Your spirit beings are all around you, but if you sleep, they will sleep."

Is that why I am dreaming this all over again? I wondered through my dream. *Has Agnes seen the lights around my self lodge dim?*

Through my dream, I remembered a telephone conversation I had with Leni Reifenstahl about six months before she passed away. I had wanted to write a book about women of power, and I considered her an extraordinary woman. Whatever her belief structures were, as a female she was quite something. She had been diving in British New Guinea, hundreds of feet below the surface with diving tanks that she carried herself and she had discovered a new species of fish that had never been seen before. And she did this in her nineties!

I had long been fascinated with her story. My agent had discovered a way to call her and it so happened that her assistant had read my books and was thrilled with them. The assistant also, I think, convinced Leni to talk to me. I'll never forget it. Leni came to the phone and said, "Lynnie, this is Leni."

We had a wonderful conversation. She told me, as Agnes had told me, that the moon is more powerful than the sun. She said, "It's not the sun. It's the moon. Study the moon."

"Why do people say that the moon is more powerful than the sun?" I asked Agnes.

"It is passivity," she answered. "It overwhelms the world and becomes only light." She began drawing a stick figure in the sand.

"Tell me again, Agnes," I said. "Why are they called 'ghost dolls'?" It was difficult moving back and forth between my dream and my previous experience with Agnes, and in my dream I felt the need to make sure that I was at least on some kind of track.

"They are called ghost dolls because they are attached to you. That is, you force a part of your spirit to animate them. You give them life. You give them life force that comes from an unexpressed aspect of your inner self."

She once again began explaining the mourner doll to me. I watched her more closely this time, and I realized now that she had been and was speaking of something so important to her that she had moved completely out of her body. It was like her body was a shell. It was propped up in the way that she was sitting, but she had gone somewhere else.

I asked, wanting to bring her back, "But why are they ghost dolls, Agnes?"

Coming back, animating her form, she said, "Because they exist like shadows of your spirit, reminding you of your inner life."

I thought of fetishes, of the *kachinas* made by Native Americans in the Hopi reservations and different parts in the country. I saw images of these inspired carvings made out of cottonwood that has been struck by lightning, then painted and wrapped with feathers and masks, creating a representation of the unknown, the world of spirit on the other side.

After repeating what she had told me before about ghost dolls, how they represent the powers within a person, the life force, the death force, she reminded me, "What you choose not to look at in life rules your life." Agnes had begun whittling on a piece of driftwood that was full of rather ugly knots and burls. Holding it up before me, she told me, "Something like this," and I gathered that I was going to make another ghost doll. Then she stood up, pulled me up to my feet, smudged me with the sage that she had been carrying in her pocket. She blessed me with sweet grass. She put her hand on my solar plexus four times, and she said, "Get to work."

I sat back down on the sand and tried to get in touch with the male side of myself as I had experienced it before, the father, the Ancestral Father, the grandfathers who had walked the trail before me. So many accomplished, magnificent ancestors, yet very overly disciplined, overly creative, overly successful. I realized that so much had been expected of me by my father. That had been a huge issue in my life. Somehow, because he wanted perfection from me and probably from himself as a trained engineer, he was such a perfectionist that he would become still and then begin to feel unworthy.

Unworthiness is where his rage came from. I suddenly realized that. I had never seen it before. I was so close to him that all I could feel was the pain of constantly waiting for him to go into a rage and take it out on me emotionally. Those are wounds that don't show.

The first time I had been on Elkhorn Mountain with Agnes, we had talked of the sadness that I still carried, even after many years of working on it. Now I realized that it was time to go beneath that sadness. It was time to go directly into the anger that underlies such all-consuming sadness. I have never handled anger well, mine or anybody else's, and I understood that this was something I needed to look at now. Sometimes an epiphany comes to us and we see so clearly what a particular stumbling block has been all about. Sometimes our lessons are revealed to us in layers, going deeper and deeper as we become ready to grow into them.

I picked up one of my twisted roots and held it to my heart, understanding that this mourner doll was finally going to be about my anger. I closed my eyes and tried to go back to those early days, when I was only six years old. My mother was not with us at that time. She had left to find another place in Seattle to live. For two or three years, I was with my father. Every day I experienced this unsettling fear of twistedness. Nothing was pure. I couldn't see clearly enough to understand the gifts that I had. I could see lights around my father while he was having a rage, red light all around him. Then the light would dissipate. I sensed that my ability to see lights around people meant something, but I didn't know what.

At the point that the red light dissipated, my father likely would have had me up all night, blaming everybody, mainly his parents, for all of the issues that troubled him. I could never help him and I could never be a child. I was twisted. I was twisted around my own feelings of terror, wanting to be free and yet not knowing how to find the sun, the illumination I so desperately needed.

The twig that I was holding was so twisted it looked dried up and tortured in the way that it had grown. And I thought, *Those are the things that I had to overcome*. . when I went to college, when I left home. Those were the things that I carried around for years and years. Still, there was a shadow of that. That's why the twig, the root that no longer continues to grow. You let it dry in the sun. You use it as kindling, and let it be washed away by the river. Those were the feelings. They hadn't gotten washed away. They were left behind, like this little twig.

Holding the twig felt like I had felt with my father. I began to build my doll. It wasn't going to look like my other mourner doll had looked. When I finished, I wrapped everything up in a bandana and headed off to find Agnes. I already felt better. Having taken out of me these feelings that I have always carried, putting them into something tangible that I could feel and look at, had already helped me and lightened my load. I felt lighter, more free.

Circling Back: "The Healing Power of Forgiveness"

What does your hidden anger have to do with what you may have been unable to create for yourself in life?

When we think of anger, we so often think of fighting and war. We think of all the angry people around us, as if that anger does not live within us, too. We think of other people who have done something against what we believe in or think to be important, who have infringed on our circle of power in some way, as if our anger is their fault and their responsibility. And what, then, do we do to resolve that anger?

How do you handle your anger? Do you try to ignore it, as if that will somehow make it all better? Or do you over-react? What an enormous energy drain both of these are, leaving you deflated sometimes for days. It takes an enormous amount of our energy to carry our anger around with us, regardless of whether we are trying to pretend we are not angry or are plotting our revenge. In my situation with my father, I had buried my anger so deeply inside of me at such a young age that for years, I didn't know it was there. I just knew that I never quite felt that I fit into my own life, and the Sisterhood saw this. I was able to get angry in a given situation, but I had walls around my deep anger that were blockading me, and I didn't see it.

Think about where anger lives in your body. Close your eyes for a moment and feel where anger, where holding the word 'anger' or the thought of anger, lives in your body. Then make a mental note and imprint it on this part of your body. This is something you want to heal before it grows into something you do not want in your life. Anger can be like a flame. It can be the other side of passion, motivating you. Or it can paralyze you completely. The choice is yours. Neither your anger nor what it was that made you so angry has anything to do with how you choose to respond to your anger. Think about it.

The story I most often use to illustrate this is when Agnes Whistling Elk asked me to come and live with her in the far north of Canada for a few years. I put everything I had in storage, rented out my house, and I went to Canada with such excitement and abandon, only to be told by her, "No. What are you doing here? You don't belong here."

At first, I thought she was kidding. When I realized she was serious, I started crying.

She had just told me, essentially, to 'stuff it.' She had told me that I was to go back home (*Right, Agnes, to the house I just rented out, yes?*), take the things that the women of the Sisterhood had taught me (*Would that be the things you have told me I am never to share with anybody because I'm not even supposed to know you?*), and, "Let the eagles fly. Take what you have learned and share it. Take the ancient and sacred way of woman back to your people. Go home."

I was unbelievably furious, and this was just what Agnes had wanted. She wanted me to be as angry as she could make me. And the reason was because she knew I was a wounded child. As a result of that wounding, as a result of having grown up in a house filled with rage, where nothing was ever certain except that there would be more rage, it was as impossible for me to deal with my anger as it was for me to finish what I started, no matter how much it meant to me, one of the devastating consequences of holding onto unresolved anger. She knew intimately that I wanted to be an author, that I had written all of my life and that I had done absolutely nothing with my writing. I had done the beginning, but I was paralyzed when it came to the middle and the end.

She also knew that I had just rented out my house in an iron-clad lease. I had nowhere to go and no money to get there. She knew that I would become so furious that it would force me to go to work and finish the many books I had started. I was terrified of being miserable. I was more terrified of success, terrified that I would have to take my place in the world in a position of success. And what if I couldn't live up to it? I was so terrified that I was paralyzed.

So my teachers in the Sisterhood of the Shields had decided to hold up a mirror for me that I would have no choice but to look into. Mirroring is a vital teaching of the Sisterhood. A mirror is the reflection of what we are doing and saying in the moment that helps us to see clearly and understand the nature of ourselves or of a situation that is being mirrored back to us. It is a sacred tool, a device for introspection just as our body is a tool for discovering how we hold and convolute power in our lives. Our physical existence, what we are doing, thinking, feeling in the physical world and in our bodies, provides mirrors for learning. The mirror Agnes held up for me was the mirror of anger and I was on fire, fueled by my fury at what I felt was their betrayal and heartlessness.

It was this anger, of course, that made it possible for me to find the motivation that was so desperately needed for me to finish even one simple book. The situation in which I found myself was so overwhelming that it made writing a book seem simple by comparison, and I have never forgotten this lesson. It was a lesson in the good use of anger.

Anger is going to come up in our lives. Things happen and they aren't always pleasant. When anger comes, you can make good use of it or you can fall prey to it and become its victim. It is a choice that is yours to make every time something angers you.

First, however, you have to learn how to get angry. That was something that, because I had grown up in an angry household but wasn't allowed, myself, to get angry, I didn't know how to do, and the Sisterhood knew this. So they held it up as a mirror for me.

When my parents divorced, there were a couple of years when I was forced to live with my very dysfunctional father. I knew that he had forced my mother to leave and it terrified me. I was only six years old. Not only had my mother left, but we had no money. My father had spent his family fortune in very unfortunate ways, and we were eking out a living in a trailer, eating the most inexpensive foods, like Spam and sugar spread on white bread.

One day, my father had an inspiration. Afterwards, he went outside and picked up a piece of petrified wood that he had gathered in the Petrified Forest years before. He brought it into the house and said, "You know. I have an idea." He was an engineer, and an invention had come to him in the middle of the night.

"I know that I can make an engine that doesn't take fuel, a little motor that will run and create its own energy," he announced, and he set to work creating it. The idea for this new invention inspired him to act, and from that day on, we had money again. We could live.

He put the little piece of petrified wood in my hand and he said, "If you ever forget to be grateful, pick up this stone. Put your hand on this stone and be reminded that what we have is love."

Even though my father was extremely dysfunctional, he loved me very much and he worked hard to give me the understanding that I could take my power in the world, even as a woman, especially as a woman. There was that push/pull relationship. It can be so much more difficult for a woman to be powerful in a patriarchal world, and my father didn't want that for me. How can you be angry with someone who gives you so much foundation in life, even as he takes it away in the next moment? I would get angry and swallow it, get angry and swallow it . . . until the Sisterhood held up a mirror of anger for me that was so powerful I couldn't swallow it. I had to look into it, go into it, and find my way out the other side.

There is a wonderful legend of the Buddha that I first heard when I was in Nepal with Ani. A man came to Buddha one day saying terrible, hurtful, hateful things to him. The Buddha sat there, smiling and listening.

When finally the man was finished, the Buddha said to him, "Thank you."

And the man said to Buddha, "Why aren't you furious with me? I am saying horrible things to you."

"No, I am grateful," said the Buddha. "I am grateful and I am filled with forgiveness, because it is clear to me that I hurt you in another life. I have been waiting all of my life for you to come and say these things to me in order that I could complete that aspect of my karma, so that I can be totally free. And now you have come to me and closed the circle. We have no more karma, you and I. Say nothing more."

It is extremely difficult for people in Western cultures to understand forgiveness and the laws of karma in the way of the Buddha, a forgiveness that comes out of the understanding that if someone insults you in this life, most likely in another lifetime you insulted that person.

It is, however, as the Buddha said. We are not free when we have not forgiven people, ourselves included, for things that have been done and not done. We also cannot be free if we are not grateful for the opportunity to right past wrongs, no matter how difficult that may be.

Sometimes it seems impossible to understand forgiveness, at all. So often when I work with people who have been deeply wounded, we get to the point where the only thing left to heal is their relationship with forgiveness over what has happened, and they balk. They get angry all over again and don't know how to move off that miserable stump. I understand. They are not alone on that stump. We live in a very angry world.

We have developed such a tortured relationship with forgiveness. Somehow we have come to look at it as akin to saying, "Oh, it's alright what that person did. It doesn't matter. I forgive them."

And that is utter nonsense. No wonder we have such a problem with forgiveness. The reality is that what happened may matter a great deal. You may have sustained real harm, and that needs to be healed. It made you angry, and that also needs to be healed. But revenge has never and will never heal anger. Please remember that.

Before you can heal anything, however, you must take a very important step. You must look at your own ego. If your ego was in some way threatened, probably it left you seething inside. Our egos get us into more trouble, even, than our fear of dying, which is huge. Just look at the angry world around you and how much ego you see reflected in that anger.

So look at your ego and the energy its anger is robbing from you. Then look at what this anger of yours is keeping you away from in your life. Ask yourself, "Okay, what's more important to me? Appeasing my ego? Or finding out how I can resolve the anger so that I can move on with my life, heal the situation that happened to me in ways that really are good for me?"

That was why the Buddha was able to be so solicitous of the man. The Buddha had no ego invested in him in any way.

It is a fundamental truth that forgiveness must be reached for there to be real healing in your life, and forgiveness can be terribly elusive if ego is involved, more accurately, if the ego mind is involved.

Ego is an important aspect of a healthy consciousness. It helps us to know and honor our own personal truth in life. It helps us to move through life with a positive sense of ourselves. If you have a healthy ego, you don't take it personally when things go wrong. Instead, you focus on fixing what is yours to fix, asking for help when you need it and giving help wherever you can, and you trust that there is a greater plan for all of us that is beyond the limits of our own vision. You are willing to be wrong, and you give other people the same right to be wrong. You are willing to weigh the thoughts and words of others when you disagree.

You certainly don't need to be right all of the time in order to feel good about yourself.

You know that your ego is not healthy when it is constantly telling you how fabulous you are in comparison to everybody else: "They"ve got it all wrong. "They" don't understand your true genius. "They" are just too stupid. "Somebody" has to pay for what has happened to you and that "somebody" isn't going to be you.

That is when you know you have moved into self-importance, which comes from the ego mind, not the ego. It is the ego mind that tells you stories about how much better you are than what others are willing to give you, tells you that you are better than those around you, more entitled to succeed.

There is an attachment that happens when you move into self-importance, a certain kind of energy dynamic. Old sorcerers call it "the devils." They say that when you are wrapped up in your own self-importance, you have devils sitting on top of your head. These devils, however, are not evil spirits from some foreign source. They are of your own making. They are shadow dwellers, creations of your own negativity that will devour you and destroy your life if you feed them often enough.

So when you are dealing with your anger, it is vital that you first look at where it is coming from. Is it coming from your ego mind? If so, back out of there right now. It will only lead you down roads you truly don't want to follow.

I would like to offer a somewhat different perspective on forgiveness. If you look up "forgive" in the dictionary, this is what you will find: *"Forgive: to give up resentment of . . . ."*

Stop and think about how truly healing it is to give up your resentment. When you are in resentment, you are in real darkness and it is a dangerous place to be. Resentment has a very big mouth. It will consume you if you let it. It will devour your life and everything you've ever dreamed life could be, especially if you follow it down the pathway to revenge. Revenge, finding someone to pay for what was done to you, isn't going to heal you in any way. There are times others do have to pay for a wrong they have inflicted, but fortunately, especially in the most serious cases, we live in a world where there are institutions for just that purpose. So let them do their job. Your task is to heal your wounds. Focusing on revenge is only going to fuel your resentment. There is another path to follow, a path that takes you into the light of healing grace. It is the pathway of gratitude. You can't come to the healing grace of forgiveness, the letting go of resentment, until you first come to gratitude.

Being grateful is a celebration of the life force. It is a celebration of light, a way of saying to the Great Spirit, "Thank you for the great gifts of life. Thank you for all of the things that have gone *right* in my life today," instead of, "Blast the world for all of the things that have gone wrong." You take the focus of your attention off whatever it was that went wrong and you place it on all of the things that *didn't* go wrong, all of the things that are right in your life. Let that focus open your heart to a celebration of thankfulness to God for the great gifts of life, and allow the healing grace of forgiveness to fill you.

When you focus on what you have to be grateful for instead of your resentment for wrongs perceived or real, so often you find that all of the barbs and arrows simply fall away. Where there has been real harm, it is only when you let go of the destructive force of resentment that your life can begin to heal. You reverse the feeling of resentment to a position of love for yourself, love for life, love for something or someone important to you. This love moves you into the energy of forgiveness. That is when you can allow the life force of the Great Spirit to flow into you and heal you.

In the teachings of my teachers, whenever you have experienced a deep wounding, the only way to heal the wound is to go right into the heart of it. Don't ignore it. You don't relive it, but you also don't discount it or deny it thinking that the ill feelings will just go away. That way of thinking just keeps you locked in the wound.

Go into the heart of the wound and learn its lessons. Discover what it can teach you about yourself and your life, and become grateful for the chance to heal and grow and learn. Perhaps it shows you that you have more strength and endurance than you have ever credited yourself for having. Perhaps it shows you for the first time that your courage and your creativity in moving on with your life are true and beautiful forces of nature just waiting for you to become aware of them.

When you discover the lessons that the wound holds for you, you move into forgiveness. You are able to give up the resentment because you have found something so much better to replace it.

Make your life about celebrating forgiveness, not fueling resentment!

Then you realize that while you may not be happy with what happened, you can be profoundly grateful for what you have learned about yourself and your life because of it. You realize you may have never found spiritual growth and contentment without going through what you did just went through.

Today, when something makes me as angry as my father used to, I hold the piece of petrified wood that he gave me and I think about what the Sisterhood taught me by throwing me into a situation that made me so angry and terrified that it was either move through it or drown in a festering sea of poisoned dreams. Not only did they teach me to get angry, they taught me how to deal with that anger in a healthy, constructive way.

They knew, because I had told them so many times and had faced down so many of their earlier trials, that the one thing I wanted more than anything else in the world was to continue my work with them. So they told me to go away and learn how to write my books, which was always my first passion in life, from beginning, middle, and end, and then begin again. Then and only then could I come back to them, when I had my first book in hand.

I could have done other things with my anger, but I had come too far to go back down those terribly self-destructive roads. Anger is what made it possible for me to find the motivation that was so desperately needed to stare down my terror of actually writing a book and risking the possibility that I might become successful. I have never forgotten that. My anger finally motivated me to move forward in my life, honoring a talent I knew I had but didn't know how to trust, and that moved me into being able, finally, to forgive my father and really let go of the past.

When you find yourself in a fit of anger, don't focus on the anger, as tempting as that may be. If danger is present, get yourself out of harm's way. Acknowledge your feelings, the fear, the hurt, the anger, perhaps the betrayal and loss, but don't dwell on them; they are poison. Instead, look for the things that are right in your life at that very moment, like the fact that you were able to get out of harm's way. Follow that thread into the magnificent things you have been given in your life, your talents, your ability to think and reason, your intrinsic beauty. Look to them and find gratitude. Let that gratitude move you into the healing power of forgiveness, the healing power of letting go of resentment instead of fueling it. Instead of following the trail of anger, follow the trail of gratitude as it leads you toward forgiveness and true healing. You are worth it.

12

A FAIRY TALE

THE GREAT SPIRIT IS CLOSE to us but we are often so far from Spirit. Silver Tongued Coyote trotted across downed trees that formed bridges over meadow creeks, watching the sparkling secrets reflected by the turning Aspen leaves.

She came to an old oak tree in a beautiful meadow. She had never been there before but thought this might be a good place to take a little nap, tucked safely beneath a mighty oak tree. Coyotes prefer dens, and there was an inviting indentation between the tree's huge roots made just for coyotes. She was just about to fall asleep when a very strange fellow tumbled out of the tree, startling her. There hadn't been any whiff of the scent of another living being when Coyote approached the tree. Curiously, there was no scent now.

The strange fellow dangled just above the ground looking wooden and incorrigible as he tried to kick himself free of the branches. He held a sightless mask over his face and hooted at Coyote's astonished look. The apparition appeared to be a marionette attached to beaded and feathered strings hanging from the storm clouds of heaven. Who knew who pulled them or made him dance in such an animated fashion?

Finally freeing himself of the branches, the wooden fellow dropped to the ground and took off his mask. Beneath it was a long-nosed face with huge ears.

"Unbelievable," Silver Tongued Coyote said.

"Just so," said the fellow, looking quite pleased with himself.

"Why is your nose so long? You could hang rings on it," Coyote remarked.

"So many lies we tell ourselves. So many lies," the strange fellow said as he turned to leave.

"Lies, what lies?"

"My ears seem to grow when people lie to me, or when I say to myself how beautiful my nose is when I know that it isn't," the boy said, evading the question as he turned back to look intently at the coyote. Coyote thought she saw the boy's ears grow a little bit, but she wasn't sure. "I hear their lies," the wooden boy continued, "and I know them to be lies. I hear them say things like, 'I'm right and you're wrong,' and I can't bear it. And my ears grow." He started to cry, then stopped. "They are so beautiful, don't you think?" He stroked his ears gently and danced a jig, and it seemed to the coyote that the ears shrank just a little bit.

Coyote didn't know what to say. This character before her looked like a vision out of the children's book she had once heard being read aloud to a couple of small children. *Pinocchio*, or something like that.

"Are you Pinocchio?" Coyote finally asked.

"I am not," declared the strange fellow. "I'm a real boy." He was indignant, as both his nose and his ears seemed to grow.

"I'm sorry. You look like a puppet to me." Coyote watched in fascination as the fellow's ears seemed to grow a little.

"You're a very strange-looking coyote, yourself," the fellow said.

Coyote became instantly self-conscious about her long tongue. To trick the strange fellow so he couldn't see the tongue, she wrapped it around her throat like a muffler. Wooden Boy moved closer to the coyote, the rivets holding his joints together shining copper in the sunlight. He looked at Coyote's muffler, this way and that, and finally reached out and poked it with a wooden finger.

"Ouch!" Coyote growled, backing away, and she began to trot around the strange fellow in a rather stiff-legged fashion.

"That's your tongue!" Wooden Boy said. "What makes it so terribly long?" he asked, giggling to himself.

"You have a long nose and big ears and I have a long tongue," Coyote said. "So what?" Her eyes narrowed to slits and she growled under her breath.

"Let me see, let me see!" Wooden Boy said, jumping up and down.

Slowly the coyote unfurled her tongue, which flared down onto the ground. One side of it was pierced with diamonds and glittering things. The other side had lacy pieces and was silver.

"Oh, my heavens," Wooden Boy said, holding his hands over his ears. "You . . . you . . . you're the silver-tongued devil, the Coyote Trickster."

"I am not," Coyote said. "I am a real coyote, thank you."

"Well, real or not, that's who you are. You're the Coyote Trickster."

"Hmph," Coyote said as her tongue grew a little longer. She felt sly and tricky as she looked at the wooden boy's arm, which seemed like a perfect chew toy.

"No you don't," Wooden Boy said, reading Coyote's thoughts. "If we don't respect each other, I'll take my leave right now." Suddenly his strings had tightened and he was dangling below a dancing cloud, and the coyote felt lonely. She liked her new friend, even if he was a very strange fellow.

"Come back. Come back," Coyote said. "I'm sorry. I promise to behave."

"Alright." Wooden Boy dropped back to earth slowly, moving his arms and legs, and the two stood looking at each other.

"I guess we like each other, huh?" Coyote said.

"You're awfully weird," Wooden Boy said as Coyote threw her tongue over one shoulder for warmth. The two talked a little longer, making plans to meet back at the oak tree the next day. Then they walked off in different directions, leaving no trace of themselves behind.

The following day found me sitting under the oak tree, writing in a little note pad descriptions of some of the birds that were flying around. A young rabbit nibbled on the wild grass in the green dappled sunlight. All of a sudden I saw something very unusual coming up over the hill. I wasn't sure what it was, but as it drew closer I realized that it was a marionette with strings reaching up into the clouds. I had no idea who was moving him, but here he came.

What in the holy world is going on here? I wondered, shaking my head to make sure I wasn't dreaming. Or maybe I was? I didn't know what kind of tea it was that Agnes and I had shared before I left for my walk. Sometimes different teas make me drowsy. I didn't feel sleepy. Indeed, I was fascinated with this fellow approaching me.

"Hi," I said as he walked right up to me.

"Hello," he replied, sounding a bit put out. "I was supposed to meet somebody here, but he, or she, didn't show up. Here you are, instead."

"Well," I said, "what can I do for you?"

"I guess I'm lost," the wooden boy said. "Maybe I came to the wrong oak tree. You haven't seen a coyote with a long silver tongue, have you?"

I leaned back wondering what was happening here. I said, "Why don't you sit down? What is your name?"

"I am a real boy," he said. "I know I look like Pinocchio, but I'm not. My name is Real Boy."

"Well, hello Real Boy." I looked at him as he sat down, his joints creaking. His nose somehow looked a little bit longer than when he first appeared. The rivets holding his arms and legs together were shining in the reflected sunlight.

I thought, *This is the strangest thing I've ever seen and I must do something.*

"I know that it's shocking to see me," Real Boy said, interrupting my thoughts. "But I can think just like you and I'm a really wonderful person, and I can do whatever you need me to do. I can be your friend."

So I said, "Well, then. Let's be friends. So, Real Boy, what would you like to do?"

And he said, "I don't want to be made out of wood and rivets any more. They are all getting old and squeaky and it upsets me. I want very much to understand why I am in this position. There was once an old man who told me lots of things. He was a carpenter, and he told me all about the kind of wood I was made out of and what a fine piece of wood it really was." I noticed that not only did his nose grow when he said certain things, his ears also seemed literally to grow and shrink as he was speaking.

He stopped talking and a little breeze came up from the west, lifting the flowers in the field, little yellow daisy-like flowers of blue and white. I took a deep breath and watched him for a while. I couldn't help but notice his sadness.

"You feel very separate and different, don't you?" I asked.

"No," he said quickly. "I'm just disappointed that my friend didn't show up like he said he would. Well, perhaps I am separate and different," he said scratching one big ear. "How could I possibly feel otherwise? There is just nothing that I can explain." I noticed that his nose also seemed to grew and shrink as he spoke, but I thought perhaps it was best not to say anything.

"You know, Real Boy," I said instead, "all any of us is, really, is consciousness." A little blue robin's egg fell out of its nest in the oak tree and landed softly on the lush grass. "We have a form," I said, gesturing to the egg, "but we are not form. We are consciousness. This egg is formed holding a tiny baby bird that knows exactly what it will be. Your complaint is about your form, not about your consciousness. Maybe we should work on your consciousness a little," I offered as I climbed up in the tree to put the little egg back in its nest.

"I don't care about that," Real Boy answered. "I don't care about my form at all. I am just tired of being so rigid. That's how I was made, rigid like a plank."

Then he got up and started to do a little jig around the tree. I noticed that both his nose and his ears grew a little. "See, I'm better than you think, aren't I? I'm really not so bad, I'm really fun."

I looked at him and said, "Yes, you are fun. So, are you telling me that you don't really care about your form?" I was thinking that he wasn't made to be rigid at all. He had joints and rivets in all the right places, and I suspected that he could make more moves than I could, if he tried.

"Oh, yes, I do. I care very much about my form. I just don't want to admit it," he said. It looked like his ears shrank just a bit, maybe his nose, too, but I couldn't tell for certain.

"I see," I responded. "You are unhappy with your physical form but you don't want to admit it. So what do you think you should do about this?"

"I don't like this conversation," Real Boy said. "I wish the coyote I met yesterday was here instead of you. She didn't ask me so many questions. And she had a funny-looking long, silver tongue. I thought maybe I had finally found somebody I could play with, even if she was just a coyote."

"Well, think about this," I said as Real Boy sat down on the grass. Frankly, I had expected him to leave. "Is it possible that you really are the result of what you think you are? That maybe in this lifetime you've never taken the initiative to create your form properly, if that's truly what you are so upset about?"

"I don't know," said Real Boy. There was an edge to his voice. "I don't know anything, so how can I know what I'm supposed to create?"

"Why don't we go over to the pond?" I asked Real Boy, noticing that his ears had grown somewhat larger.

"I don't want to," Real Boy said, pouting. "I'm supposed to meet somebody else here instead of you. Maybe she's standing me up. Who knows? I thought we were going to be very good friends, you know. But she is the silver tongued devil and I think maybe she's a sorcerer. That's a scary thought," he said to himself.

"Does she do bad things?" I asked.

"How should I know?" Real Boy answered. "I just met her yesterday. But I think it's a bad thing that she made me believe she wanted to be my friend and then didn't bother to show up like she promised." With that, he lay back on the grass, pointed to the leaves on the tree and began counting.

"I've heard it said that some of the old shamans say a sorcerer never kills you. He makes you kill yourself, out of terror, usually, but maybe just because he makes you feel so badly about yourself. That would be a good thing to remember if you have a friend who has those leanings," I said.

Real Boy ignored me, but I noticed that he was no longer counting leaves and his ears had gotten a little bit smaller. "I thought you were going to the pond," he said after a long period of silence. He sounded very irritated, and from the way he was looking around anxiously, I wondered if he might have heard something I'd missed.

"Let's do it, then," I said, putting my pen and notepad in my bag and standing up.

"I don't want to," he replied, but as I approached the pond I noticed that he was trailing just a couple of feet behind me. I picked out a very big rock and sat down on it. He picked out an even bigger rock and sat down on it after looking to see how far he was from the water. I got the sense that he didn't much want to get wet. I picked up a stick and began twirling it through the water. Then I threw a pebble into the middle of the pond, causing the water to ripple out in multiple circles.

"Did you ever stop to think that when you have a thought, any kind of thought, it ripples out just like that water in the pond? That it affects not only you but every single person or creature around you?" I asked.

He didn't answer me, but he did roll his eyes skyward and say to a passing cloud, "Like that's anything wondrous or new."

"Why are you in such a bad mood?" I asked. A chilly north wind began blowing out of nowhere. I took my beautiful silver muffler out of my bag and put it around my throat.

Real Boy's eyes widened and he looked at me strangely. "What are you doing?" he asked.

"I'm putting my scarf on, what do you think?"

"Nothing. I don't think anything. It's just that your scarf reminds me of somebody," he said. I thought I saw his ears begin to grow and then change their mind, if that was possible.

"Well, that's good, I guess," I replied.

Real Boy lapsed back into a sullen silence, but I noticed him stealing alarmed glances at my beautiful silver neck scarf when he didn't think I was watching. He tried to whistle, but it was difficult for him to form his mouth in a whistling sort of way. Instead, he began singing a little ditty about how "some people" seemed to think he was being a smart aleck when all he was trying to do was not be frightened, and how hard would it be for "some people" to offer a little help once in awhile instead of asking stupid questions and lecturing to him.

I noticed that his nose grew a little bit longer with each "some people" refrain of his, but I didn't think he was aware of it. It didn't seem there was anything I could say to him at the moment, so I went back to tapping my stick on the water's surface and trailing it through the ripples.

"How hard would it be for some people to just accept somebody who only wants to be accepted, instead of trying to fill his head with a bunch of useless thoughts?" he asked, looking away from me.

When I didn't respond, he tried again. "'Some people' don't even want to talk to me," he said, looking at his reflection in the pond. "And quite frankly, I don't want to look like this," he said, grabbing one of his ears and trying to wiggle it up and down. It didn't wiggle, but it did shrink a little bit.

"'Some people' want to make you believe that everything that's wrong is all your fault," he continued after a bit, squeezing his ears.

I finally said, "Well, Real Boy. If you want to change the way you look, what is keeping you from changing the way you look? What is keeping you from shape-shifting into the real boy you really want to be?"

"I knew it. I knew it. I knew it all along. You're a sorcerer. Talk to me about 'shape-shifting'. I should have known there was something off about you long before you put on that ugly silver scarf." With that, he reached over and poked a finger into my scarf.

"Ouch!" I exclaimed, pulling back.

I lapsed back into silence, looking at Real Boy out of one eye and then the other.

"What are you doing?" he asked, almost crying.

"I'm just looking at you. Have you ever noticed that things look one way when you look at them with both eyes. You look at them with only one eye and they appear a little different. Then you look at them with only the other eye, and they look different still."

He didn't say anything, but shortly thereafter I noticed he was looking at his legs with first one eye and then the other.

"It's your consciousness, you know," I said.

"What do you mean by that?" he asked.

"Well, your consciousness is how you think underneath everything, inside you, the hidden part, the secret part of you trying to understand what it is you really want. When you don't look at yourself as you really are, you aren't respecting yourself," I said.

"I respect myself," he said. I didn't bother to look at what his nose and his ears did.

"No you don't," I replied. "You don't even like your reflection in that pond."

He looked at himself and said, "Ugh, no, I don't. That long nose and these big ears . . . I just look stupid."

"Well if that's what you think, then that's what you will be," I said. "Why do you have such a long nose?"

He said, "Because, well . . . I have noticed that if I tell a lie or a fib . . . ."

"Um hum," I nodded. "And your ears?" I asked.

Real Boy was polishing one of the rivets on his knee the same way I rub my legs when I am cold. I crossed to his rock, unwound the end of my muffler, watching Real Boy eye it nervously, and put it over his knee even though I strongly suspected that he didn't really feel cold. He was just mimicking me.

"Thank you," he said sincerely.

"What were we talking about?" I asked.

"We were talking about my nose," he said.

"Well, you really do have a long nose," I said with a laugh.

He couldn't help but laugh and he stroked his nose, saying, "Oh heavens, it's bigger than it was. I must have told you some lies." With that, his nose shrank a good bit.

"And what about your ears?" I asked, pressing my luck. "Why do they seem to grow bigger and smaller, depending on what you are thinking and saying?"

Real Boy looked at me as if I had struck him, and I was afraid he was about to topple over into the water.

"I . . . well, I, I . . . I do notice that when I tell myself it doesn't matter how I look, people should just love me anyway, my ears tend to shrink a little" he said.

"That's the truth," I said earnestly. "People should love you anyway. But do you want to know why they don't?" I asked, throwing a pebble into the pond and watching the ripples shining in the sunlight. The wind died down and I undid the rest of my muffler from around my neck, which disturbed Real Boy terribly.

"Oh, my," he exclaimed, alarmed. "Would you stop doing that?"

I said, "Okay, I didn't mean to disturb you."

"Well you did," he said with finality.

I said, "Let's get back to our conversation. You were saying that you really don't mind looking like you do, but you also want to fit in and you think your looks make that impossible. Therefore, you don't want to look like yourself. Which is it? Your consciousness doesn't know what you are saying, so your consciousness does not know what to create."

Shaking his hands back and forth, Real Boy said, "Ohhhhh, wait a minute. I don't know what you are talking about. That's way too hard for me to understand. Are you crazy or something? Maybe you are. You are sitting here talking to me, after all."

I put my arms around his little shoulders, and it felt like I was holding an armful of sticks. After a moment, he said, "Thank you. Nobody ever holds me."

And I said, "Well, that's a terrible thing. It's interesting, when you say something true about yourself, your ears get smaller."

"What else are we going to talk about?" he asked.

"Well," I said, "you tell me. You don't like your nose. You don't like your ears. It seems to me that those are things you can directly control, but you don't want to talk about that. What about the strings you have on you, that seem to make you move? Do you know who it is that is pulling on them?"

And he said, "Well, that is sort of a problem. Sometimes when I want to move, whoever is pulling those strings doesn't want me to move."

And I said, "So, besides everything else, the big nose and the big ears, you don't know who is pulling your strings."

"I guess not," he said. Both his ears and his nose grew a little bit and he looked away.

I replied, "That's kind of an interesting thing, isn't it? So where is your responsibility in any of this?"

"I don't know. I am so confused. And stop playing with that scarf, please. It makes me very nervous."

At that point, I said, "Come on. Let's get up and walk around the pond. It's so beautiful."

As we walked around the pond, I said to him, casually, "You see. When you want to walk, you can. That means that you do have a sacred will after all. The strings are following you, not pulling you in a different direction. They're not making you go in the water, for example. They are simply helping you to stand upright so that you can get to where you want to be. What a wonderful thing!"

He tilted his head in a reflective pose and said, "Well, you might be right. But once in a while they pull me into the clouds and I can't figure that out. I try to see who's pulling them, but I never see anybody. There is just a lot of light."

"And are you afraid of that?" I asked.

"I'm afraid when I don't know what's going on," he said. "My life is strange enough. When I suddenly get yanked into the clouds for no reason, and there is no one there, it scares me. Could you help me? I think you know things." His nose and his ears both got a little smaller.

By then we were walking through the rushes at the end of the pond, where cattails swayed in the breeze. The rushes made beautiful sounds as we walked through them. The ground was a bit wet and the screws in Real Boy's feet started to squeak a little bit.

He said, "Oh I need to get out of this water. This isn't good for me."

I steered him over to where the ground was dry but there were still rushes.

"I will help you," I said, knowing he would be an unusual subject. But I liked him.

We were walking slowly, holding the rushes apart as we walked.

I asked him, "Do you really want to change your form?"

And he answered, "I mostly like my nose, really."

"Why?" I asked.

"First of all, I get a lot of attention. Everybody wants to know why I have such a long nose."

"But you said people didn't like you because of your nose." I noticed a beautiful robin flying overhead and watched as it flew directly to the nest I had discovered in the oak tree. I was glad that she had come back and thought that the little bird in that egg had a very good chance.

"Well, I don't know. Maybe they do but maybe I just think they don't. That could be," he said.

We came to a weeping willow tree with branches flowing almost to the ground. It created the most marvelous lodge, not unlike the dreaming lodge my teachers had given me up in Canada.

"Let's sit under this tree," I said to Real Boy. "It makes me feel protected. I can see the beautiful pond and hear the wind singing through the willow's branches, but I don't have to be right out in the middle of everything. Isn't it beautiful?"

As he said, "Yes it is," his ears got a little smaller.

"Did you notice what your ears just did?" I asked him. "When you speak your feelings truthfully, your ears get smaller. When you say things about yourself that aren't true, they get bigger. At least it seems that way to me."

Real Boy rubbed his wooden fingers over his cheek and said, "Well, that could be. I always figured they grew because of all the lies everybody else tells. But when I talk to you, they don't get bigger or smaller when you say things, only sometimes when I answer you."

"Let's do a little test," I said. I wanted to giggle, but I didn't want to offend Real Boy, so I just let the sparkle in my eyes say it all. "Your ears are very big. That means you are an elephant."

Real Boy laughed and laughed and his ears grew smaller, because he knew it wasn't true and for once didn't try to make himself fit into what someone had said.

"Maybe, just maybe you can learn something here," I said kindly. "Do you mind if I touch your nose, please?"

"Well, it's okay but just be careful," he said.

So I stroked his nose and I looked at him and said, "This is a beautiful nose. It is so beautifully carved. You are very lucky."

"Why am I lucky?" Real Boy said. "It makes me look funny." His ears began to twitch.

"So you are telling me you want to be just like everybody else after all. Is that what you are telling me?"

He thought about it for a moment and said, "Well, not really. I don't want to be like everybody else because then . . . well . . . then I would just be like everybody else and that wouldn't be any fun, would it?"

"No," I said, "it wouldn't be any fun at all."

The sun started to lower in the sky and it shined right into our eyes, so we moved around to the other side of our tree. Real Boy's little rivets were shining and I said, "You know, you are beautifully made. You are such a beautiful boy. Would you think for a moment that maybe that's special?"

"Not really," he said immediately. A few minutes later, he said, "Well, maybe."

"If you had your druthers and the Great Spirit . . . ," I started to say.

"Who's the Great Spirit?" he asked, interrupting me.

"Well, God is the way many people speak of the Divine Spirit. Whoever you think of as God, whoever made you, created the wood out of which you were made. A being of light, a divine force." Real Boy wasn't saying anything. He looked angry, but I wasn't sure what had triggered it, the thought of the Great Spirit or the thought of "whoever made" him. So often when people are in hate with their lives, they intentionally push all thoughts of a divine good out of their minds.

"Would you like to talk to the Great Spirit with me?" I asked, changing my approach.

"I don't know," he mumbled. "Never tried. Never really knew it was possible."

So I said, "Well, let's try. Close your eyes and breathe very deeply about three or four times while I ask the Great Spirit to take a walk with us. There's a dense woods over there, and I think it would be very good to leave all our thoughts here under the willow tree and just walk through those woods."

"I don't know," Real Boy said. "Lots of bushes are crowded together in there. I usually stay out of places like that." But as I stood, he gave me a hand so that I could help him stand, also, and we walked over to the woods. Before entering, we stopped briefly.

"Just breathe deeply and regularly," I instructed him. "Close your eyes and visualize yourself walking down a trail in these woods. Just for a few minutes, breathe deeply and see how that feels for you. Okay, now open your eyes. How did you feel about that? Did you like seeing yourself walking?"

"Well, I guess, sort of," he said. "I was going somewhere, not just standing still."

So I said, "Okay. Then let's take a little walk through these woods. Keep breathing deeply and evenly, and look at the beauty that is all around you. As you walk, try to visualize your form changing into the flesh-and-blood little boy you think you want to be. Become that boy, not a beautifully carved wooden boy. You have flesh and bones, no more rivets and wood. And we are walking together down the path."

After a time, he said, "Gosh, yeah! This is cool. But my feet hurt. I think I have a blister, and I've never had a blister before."

"Well, and what else is happening?" I asked.

He said, "I feel good but I'm still sad."

I replied, "Well, let's change that. Keep walking, and start saying to yourself, 'I'm a happy real boy and that's what I've always wanted to be. I am a happy real boy."

He repeated that and I said, "Repeat it again."

And he repeated it and then he went silent. He was walking.

"Ah, my foot hurts again, and I just scratched myself on that tree," he said. "Oh dear, I'm bleeding. I've never bled before. My foot hurts and I've never bled before. Now what do I do?" he asked.

I took a band-aid out of my pouch as I said, "We put a band-aid on your blister, like this." He picked up his foot and I put the band-aid over the blister and looked at the scratch on his arm. He had really gashed himself, so I took a little alcohol swab out of my pouch and rubbed it on the cut.

"Ouch, that hurts. It's awful!" he yelled. I knew that it would only sting for a minute or two, so I sat back on my heels and closed my eyes, waiting to see what he would do next. When I felt him begin to relax next to me, and I opened my eyes to discover that he had already started walking through the woods once again.

He only went about twenty paces before he turned to me and said, "I can't do this anymore, this flesh-and-blood thing. I don't like bleeding. My arm hurts, my feet hurt. I've never felt anything like this before. I'm getting a headache, which I've never had before, and my tummy aches."

I said, "Well, are you sure you want to leave your beautifully crafted wooden form behind? Maybe you'd like to be in it again, for a little while, so your foot doesn't hurt and you don't get scratched and you don't feel sad."

"That's a good idea because this really hurts," he said.

So I said, "Okay, then. Think with your shaman center."

"My what?" he gulped.

Taking his hand gently in mine, I placed it on his belly button and said, "Press gently. Now, bring your thoughts down to your belly button and think with your intent, that part of you that sees what needs to be done and wants to make it happen. Think with your intent that you really want to go back to the form you had before. You want to be wooden boy once again."

"Okay. Alright, because I am bleeding and I don't like this. And I'm cold. I've never been cold before," he said.

Before you know it, he was walking back down the path towards the edge of the woods and the willow tree. He was back to being a wooden boy and his nose and ears had shrunk considerably. When we sat back down under the protective covering of the willow, he looked at me and said, "You know, as a wooden boy, nothing ever hurt me like that. I didn't rub against things. Once in a while I might break a stick on my journeys, but it could always be replaced. I simply removed the rivets and put a new piece in. I did that once when I fell on the ground off a big rock."

He grew silent and thought for a long time. Finally, he said, "You know what? Thank you. I have just learned something. I think I love myself, and I've never felt that before. Just one experience of being a real boy. I don't want to get hurt like that. I think maybe it is better for me to be a wooden boy."

I said, "Well, you think about that. Think about what you are saying."

Night had fallen, so I pulled a blanket out of my pack and said, "Let's roll out the blanket and sleep for awhile, okay?"

He said, "Yes, I'm really, really tired. That took a lot of energy. I don't know if I ever want to do that again."

So saying, we both fell asleep. I woke up long before he did and greeted Mother Earth, Father Sky, Great Spirit and the powers of the four directions, thanking them for the dawning of another exquisite day. Wooden Boy was sleeping so soundly. I looked at the feathers and beads tied to his strings, and I thought, *Hmmmmm, Wooden Boy looks like he is being controlled by somebody else, but I don't think he really is. He just doesn't think he can walk around on his own. A true puppet can't walk around on its own like he does. A puppet's strings have to be pulled for it to move.*

So I climbed up the tree to see if I could see who was pulling those beaded and feathered strings, and then I saw it. There were clouds over us and in those clouds was an incredible light forming golden temples and hallways leading into infinity. It was the light of thought, the light of consciousness. And of course, there was nobody pulling those strings but the light itself. There was something he needed to learn in this lifetime about giving away all of his power and becoming somebody else's puppet, and I suspected that he had learned it yesterday as he walked through the woods as a true "real boy." I wondered what would change for him, now that he had seen and accepted himself as he truly is and wants to be in this life?

I thanked the Great Spirit for this wonderful opportunity to walk with Real Boy and talk with Real Boy, to become a mirror for him to see his true reflection.

Then I turned around and trotted in little circles around the willow tree, adjusting my magnificent tongue around my neck. A beautiful silver-tongued coyote was waiting for Real Boy when he woke up.

"Oh, there you are," he said, rubbing the sleep out of his eyes. "Where have you been? I just had the most incredible experience."

Coyote said, "Really," brushing her tongue and curling it back around her neck. Then she looked at Real Boy slyly and said, "Aren't you cold? Look, there is a scarf on the ground, Real

Boy. Why don't you pick it up and wrap it around your neck to keep you warm?"

He looked a little confused and he said, "But where is the woman? She helped me so much. You know what . . . do you know what, Coyote? I'm glad I'm a wooden boy. That's my real name, you know, 'Wooden Boy.' 'Real Boy' was just a name I thought I would use. Don't you love my exquisitely carved wooden form?

"I had an incredible experience when you didn't show up yesterday," he continued. "I scratched myself and I bled. I was a real boy. I had flesh and blood and bones. I was cold, I hurt myself, and my foot hurt. You know what? I don't feel those things as Wooden Boy. I feel other things. Sometimes I hurt in a different way, like when my rivets get rusted or a piece of my wood breaks. But those can be replaced rather simply, and I don't have to walk around in pain waiting for it to happen. I don't know how to explain it, but something really weird happened and I learned that I really do love myself just as I am. I know I have a big nose, I know I have big ears, but they're really quite expertly made. And they don't have to get as big as I let them get . . . well, as I make them get, and that's the truth."

Silver Tongued Coyote stood up and said, "Let's go over and look in the pond," and trotted off. When she got to the pond, she looked at Wooden Boy and noticed that he was walking quite differently, much more sure-footed. The strings were still there, but they were loosening in the light and they seemed to be more luminous than actual, "real string" fibers. Wooden Boy seemed to be so much a part of all of existence. I lapped a little bit of water from the pond. Of course, it's difficult to lap water when you have a tongue as long as mine, but I'd figured out how to do it just fine.

Wooden Boy sat down on a rock and Coyote said, "Let's look at ourselves in this pond. See if we can see ourselves."

"Oh that would be wonderful! Let's do that. I did that yester-day and it didn't work very well. I feel like trying it again."

He looked in the pond and his ears were smaller and beauti-ful and his nose had grown much shorter. He realized something and said, "Coyote, I am really handsome. Look at me. I don't feel scratches and pain and all those things that you . . . Well, you're an animal, but animals and people feel pain in ways that I don't. You get scratched and you bleed. All these things happen to you. I feel that I'm just a different kind of wanderer, I guess."

Coyote said, "That's probably true but don't you get lonely?"

Wooden Boy said, "Why do you ask me that?"

"Well, I just wondered if maybe you missed me when I wasn't here?"

Wooden Boy swiveled around and looked at me and said, "Yes, it's true that I get lonely. I like to talk. I could just sit here all day and talk about things, tell you stories. Wouldn't that be fun? I met the most extraordinary person yesterday, a woman, and we talked about a whole lot of strange things. By the time we fell asleep, I felt that I had learned so much. Wouldn't it be great to be able to do that more often?"

Coyote said, "Well, not so much for me, but I am a different sort of creature. I am a hunter. In fact, I'm getting hungry and I have to go out and find something to eat."

Wooden Boy said, "See, I don't even have to do that. I really don't even have to sleep, although sleeping is kind of fun."

Coyote said, "If you don't mind terribly, I am going to go find something to eat. You can follow along behind me if you want, but we can't talk. That doesn't work well when you are hunting."

Wooden Boy said, "Well, you know I really loved being under that weeping willow tree. I think I'm going to go back up there and sit. The woman said something about it being a lodge, sort of protected underneath the hanging branches, and I liked that."

Coyote growled and said, "See you later."

I began sniffing the ground for a rabbit trail, anything I could find, maybe a mouse trail. Finding a promising scent, I trotted off, a very unusual sight indeed, a coyote with a silver tongue wrapped around its throat and its fur bristling. Now I was excited, I was in the hunt.

Wooden Boy went back to the tree and sat down. He looked up at all the threads that were pulling him. He pulled back a little bit. They felt different. They felt a little like lights and yet there was a sort of texture to them. He knew that something had changed and he prayed a little bit. He used the words that I had given him, "Great Spirit."

"Great Spirit," he said. "Thank you. I feel so much better and I'm so handsome and I don't need to be a real boy any more. I'm very, very happy just being me."

Suddenly he shot bolt upright. He'd been thinking about other things he could be thankful for when a new thought danced into his head. "Shape shifter." *The silver-tongued coyote talked to me about shape-shifting. Then she went away and a woman who looked an awful lot like her, right down to the silver muffler around her throat, showed up and the next thing I know, I'm no longer a wooden boy, I'm a real boy. Then the woman is gone and Coyote Trickster is back. There's something really strange going on here. Now that I think about it, I never discovered whether the coyote was a boy or a girl. I just figured that it was a she.*

It is often said that when the student is ready, the teacher will appear. The pond below Wooden Boy began to take on light in the setting sun. An instinct came to open him outwards by letting all light in, just as a solitary bee came humming down to enter a flower in a blur of pink light. Wooden Boy held within his heart the pond, the bee, the boy within his soul. He had found a new way of seeing.

Circling Back: "Embracing the Unknown"

Many years ago, Agnes Whistling Elk and I were talking about how difficult it is for people to take their power in today's world. I was looking at all of the pragmatic aspects of our complicated modern world, trying to understand where the individual might actually fit in amid the complexities of modern living, the demands on our time and resources that seem so impossible.

Agnes wasn't having any of it. She has told me often that we were never intended to live in the stress that we experience in the world today, and she has always said that it doesn't need to be this way. This is what we are choosing for ourselves.

On this occasion, she simply looked at me in that way that she does and said, "Lynn, if you speak to a person who is standing in a powerless position and ask her to take her power, she won't do it. She becomes frightened. She becomes frightened because you are implying change. She must take a step into the mystery of the unknown to become powerful, and she doesn't want to do that. She has convinced herself that it is the world outside of her that must change."

There is great truth and understanding of modern human nature in what Agnes said. We are largely frightened of the unknown because it has become so unfamiliar to us. We prefer to stay within the confines of the known world, even if it means languishing amid all of the stresses of our lives rather than stepping outside of our needs to look at what possibilities actually do exist. Someone might notice us.

Why is it that we have grown so afraid of the unfamiliar, especially when much of what is "familiar" is exactly what is blocking us in life? What has happened to the great human spirit of discovery and invention that has brought so much good into our world? Do you think it has something to do with the neediness we have accepted as a condition of modern living?

It is fundamental to the shamanic world view that power is born from the unknown. When you sit in front of Stonehenge or the great pyramids of Egypt, you understand that you are in the presence of great power, a power that comes from an unknown source, yet a power that is as undeniable as it is mysterious.

But you don't have to travel to Stonehenge or Egypt to find the mysterious world of power that already resides within you. All you have to do is become willing to venture into the unknown wilderness of your own soul, the place within where personal truth resides. This is the place where you are one with the Great Spirit and all of life, and what a tragedy for the world that the universe within is so unfamiliar to us.

When I first found Agnes Whistling Elk and Ruby Plenty Chiefs, I was filled with fear. In the beginning, I desperately wanted change, but it was the thing I feared the most. I was terrified of the unknown. As my training progressed, it became imperative that I lose this fear, that I learn how to grow beyond it and stop using it as my crutch and excuse for staying stuck in a life I did not want. My teachers showed me that if I would become willing to let go of my fear of the unknown, I could move into the sacred mystery where the miracle of existence emerges from the darkness and transforms us into the higher spirituality that we so urgently want.

Fear is so often born in the great abyss of our unfulfilled wants and what we believe our needs to be. We all experience times of need, times when we truly need help and understanding. Needs are a legitimate and inescapable part of existence. Mother Earth needs sunshine, wind, rain and so many other things to facilitate her amazing, intricate and incredible diversity of life. Flowers need a little extra help from bees. People are just the same. We need harmony and balance with our great Mother Earth. We need harmony and balance with each other—not domination over one another—in order to survive, and especially to thrive. Nothing that lives or thrives, really, is totally self-sustaining, no matter how hard we humans try.

Sometimes, however, we can get so fixated on our needs that we become completely stuck, like my sweet friend Wooden Boy. We tell ourselves scary stories about all of the terrible things that could happen to us, and we begin to look at those who won't give us what we think we need, who won't change our world to suit us, as the ones to blame for all that is wrong. We even get to the point where we think that *our* needs are the only legitimate needs in life, all of our needs and most of our wants. Whole nations do that, so why shouldn't we?

We become preoccupied with our perception of our needs and getting our own way to the point that we don't look at a situation in its totality. We don't look for what we can learn about ourselves and our process of living that is being mirrored back to us in this situation. We don't look at the full range of options that are available to us. We especially don't look at our role in it. We are boxed in by our own neediness. What happens to the quality of our lives then?

At what point do we take responsibility for ourselves? At what point do we take responsibility for what we do and don't do as well as the consequences that follow? At what point do we take responsibility for our neediness as well as for our needs? The answers to these questions could well determine the future of our entire planet. They will certainly determine how we, individually, do in life and the truth of our own well-being.

Life is all about the great adventure of living. It's about the mystery. It is the journey, <u>getting to</u> the destination, <u>not</u> the destination. The destination is something that is often beyond us, something you might never be able to attain or control. So what? What about the amazing things you discover along the journey, the other avenues that are ready to open themselves up to you? And when you do get to your destination, what do you do but embark upon another journey?

What is neediness? Neediness is what happens when you condition your entire sense of well-being on what happens in the world outside of you. Neediness is what happens when you don't take responsibility for yourself and expect everyone around you to fix your life for you. Neediness is what happens when you stand in the place of the victim, blaming someone or something else for the woes that befall you. It is the illusion that if you could have total control in your life, everything would be just fine.

If we had "total control" in our lives we wouldn't know what to do with it, and that is exactly why it isn't given to any of us.

When you are ready to bring much-needed change into your life, you discover that your wants and needs are really a matter of perspective. You can choose to see the situations of your life as somebody else's fault and somebody else's responsibility to fix, or you can choose to look at what is going on within you that makes you feel so helpless. It is when you choose to take responsibility for yourself that a gateway opens before you. It is a gateway filled with the seeds of success, harmony and your own potential that are already within you, waiting for you to cultivate them.

When you are ready for change and you take an honest look at what is driving your fears, you discover that what is really standing in your way are your own self-imposed limitations. I certainly had self-imposed limitations when I first embarked on this pathway of shamanic discovery. In order for my work with my teachers to be successful, I was forced to change how I saw myself and what I could really do in life. I had to go within myself and challenge all of my notions about living. If I thought I couldn't do something, that was exactly the thing that my teachers demanded I do. I had to change from someone who wanted power over outside circumstances to a woman who was ready to discover and take my own power within myself.

In the process, I learned that if you want to have power in your life, you must make a place within you for power to live. You do that by letting go of your neediness, the need for someone else to make things happen for you.

Power is something that you build through having faith in yourself. When you back away from your power, as I did so often when I began working with the Sisterhood, what you are really doing is expressing a total lack of faith in your own capacity. But how will you ever know what you are truly capable of doing until you take the risk and try?

As you move toward living up to your abilities, you discover that you are moving toward embracing change. That is when you step into the mystery of the unknown. Always remember this: it is in the Unknown that all of possibility resides. When you open yourself to the unknowable, to the unfamiliar, that is when the energy of what you are seeking to create flows into you and becomes part of you, as you become part of it. You step into the unknown simply by doing something you didn't think you could do.

13

BETTY FAST BEAR

ONE SPRING I WAS up in Canada with Agnes and Ruby and Betty Fast Bear. Betty Fast Bear is a woman within the Sisterhood and somebody I have never written about because she never wanted to be talked about, written about, anything.

She is very, very strong, literally as strong as a bear. She even looks like a bear, a tall woman with very broad shoulders and dark skin. As far as I know, she is full-blood Cheyenne.

We were sitting this afternoon on Agnes's porch, darning some socks and mending a skirt that Ruby loved, saying nothing. We were in rocking chairs, which Agnes loved, rocking back and forth on the old planks that creaked and made a lot of noise. Betty had her long hair tied back in a braid and then tied up again in a kind of loop that she liked to wear. There was a red ribbon in her hair which I believe had come off of her Shield some years before. She wore the red ribbon every time I had ever seen her.

As she rocked back and forth, she poked her finger with the needle. She refused to wear a thimble, so she poked her finger and then she yelped.

"Dang it," she said. "Dang it. I'd rather be in a cave with a hibernating bear than with you, Ruby."

Ruby stopped what she was doing. She had finished what she was sewing and was now pulling apart some herbs. She had an old cowboy hat pulled down almost over her forehead to shade her eyes.

She looked at Betty and said, "That is a hell of a thing to say to your best friend."

Betty said, "Yeah, isn't it."

Ruby asked, "Do you mean it?"

And Betty kicked Ruby's boot with her own. "No, I'm just mad. I am mad at the bloodletting."

"What? What are you talking about, Betty?" I asked.

Agnes started to laugh and Betty said, "I got blood all over this thing now, and it's all your fault, Ruby, all your fault. As long as you agree with me, I'll shut up."

Ruby was horrified and said, "Hey, I'm not gonna let this go by. You can at least tell us what is the matter with you, although I know you're crazy and you always have been. You should have been Betty Crazy Bear instead of Betty Fast Bear."

Then the two women really got into it. Agnes and I looked at each other and started to laugh which, of course, made the two of them madder. Finally, Agnes and I put our things aside and went inside to make some tea while Betty and Ruby had their row. It was a lovely tea, with lavender, and we brought it back out to the porch. By then, the two women were sitting together on the porch steps and Betty had her arm around Ruby, which is about the only time I have seen anybody put their arm around Ruby in a consoling way, ever.

And she was crying. Betty Fast Bear was crying. She does not cry. And Ruby was kind of snickering. I didn't know what had happened between them, but obviously they'd come to some sort of agreement.

So we all sat down again in the rocking chairs, this time Betty and Ruby facing Agnes and me in a "U" shape on the porch. The sun was setting and it was beautiful.

Betty said, "Well, now that I have ruined everything."

"Yes, you have ruined everything, but we kind of expected that," Ruby said.

We all laughed.

"Bloodletting? What do you mean by bloodletting?" I asked. I knew there was more to Betty's little tantrum than a prick of her finger.

"The state of our world. What do you mean, 'What do I mean,' stupid *wasichu*?" Betty said. It meant, literally, "'She who takes the fat.' Stupid white woman."

Ignoring her, I asked, "You mean the wars?"

"Yeah," she said.

Ruby said, "Well, thank God I've been blinded. I don't have to look at any of it."

And then I didn't know what to say. This conversation could take so many different directions, and I knew that there was some particular place that Betty wanted it to go.

Agnes had the strangest look on her ancient, beautiful craggy-lined face. She said, "I wonder if we will ever see the time again where we will have peace?"

"When did we ever have peace?" I asked. "There are wars going on in this world all of the time between different peoples."

"Yeah, but there *was* another time," Agnes said. The Native American women shook their heads and nodded.

I said, "Well, talk to me."

"Oh, you don't want to know about this," Ruby said.

I asked her, "What do you mean? I don't want to know about what?

Betty said, "It's probably too hard for you to understand."

"Betty, you are a great healer. You are one of the great dreamers. You are known by another name, of course, among most of the shamans around the world. You have traveled. You have done everything. Why, now, are you treating me this way? What is wrong with you today?" I asked.

"I pricked my finger. What do you think?" she responded.

"Oh," I shrugged in response.

"There was a time of peace," Agnes said after a long period of silence.

A breeze had come up from the west carrying the scent of grass and earth.

"There was a time on this earth and I have, I believe, Lynn, spoken with you about this before. It was the time before sand. Do you remember that? It was many years ago," Betty said.

And I answered, "Yes, I do remember the time before sand."

I was chasing around in my mind trying to remember the conversation we had had. And I remembered having lectured on that somewhere, talking about it.

Then she said, "Well, you've been in Egypt quite a bit."

"Egypt?" I asked.

And she said, "Yes, Egypt. Hello! With Amina."

I said, "Yes, what an extraordinary woman Amina is!"

"Why, is she better than we are, stronger than us, prettier than us? I think we're pretty fabulous," Betty said.

"Betty, will you just shut up," I finally said. "I really need to talk about this."

"Okay," Betty laughed. "Alright, alright."

And Ruby said, "Yes, this is a good thing."

Agnes went on, "There was a time before sand when the history was oh, so different. Before things were covered up."

"What do you mean, covered up?"

"Covered up by sand, of course," Betty said.

"Oh, yes, covered up by sand," I said. *Obviously.*

"In Egypt, there was a great labyrinth. And this labyrinth was as big as the city of Rome," Betty continued.

"The city of Rome?" I questioned.

"Well, the downtown part," she said. "There were twelve cities within that labyrinth."

"Twelve cities?"

We were all kind of shocked.

And Agnes said, "Yes, it was a huge, beautiful gathering of wisdom. And as you would think of the Library of Alexandria, there were teachings, there was wisdom. People were different then. They raised orchids, for instance, and knew the source."

I looked at Agnes and asked, "Twin Dreamers. The source of orchids, the Pleiades?"

She said, "Oh, you do remember."

And I said, "Yes, I do."

Betty said, "Seeds had to come from somewhere. Haven't you ever noticed that orchids are very different from other flowers? They do not attract you with the same scent or flourish. They are very different, fleshy."

Agnes went on. "There was a time during Atlantis and Mu, sacred Mu, where, Lynn, you spent a lot of your learning time. You love Hawaii because it reminds you of home. California, that whole part of the world. Arizona, too, but Arizona used to be the bottom of the sea, so . . . ."

And I said, ". . . So, go on. Go on. What are you talking about, the 'time before sand?'"

Agnes paused a moment. "The time before sand. Who caused the sand to blow? Who caused the sand to cover the earth? Cover the magnificent labyrinth?"

And I said, "Oh, go back to that. Talk more about the labyrinth."

Agnes drew in the dust on the boards with a stick a design not unlike the Pentagon, and explained that there were twelve different ways of wisdom.

"Before everything was buried in sand," she said, "there were twelve different ways of wisdom brought to the labyrinth by people from twelve different regions around Egypt, no doubt the areas that we now know as Syria, Egypt, Persia, perhaps the Sinai. These ways of wisdom were different from one another, each with its own understanding. But there wasn't war. People settled their differences and honored the differences between them. The people who followed these ways loved one another. They were happy. They came from cities of joy that are also buried in sand now, maybe never to be found. Every year the people would come to the Labyrinth, to one great city and share their wisdom, just as they shared their wares, the tools that they developed and the magnificent pots that they had made. I believe, Lynn, that you have several pots from that Sumarian area."

I said, "Yes, they are beautiful and very thin, as if crafted by somebody incredibly talented."

"They were a gift to you, to help you remember things. The labyrinth was a place, huge and remarkably magnificent," Agnes said.

I knew, of course, that Herodotus, called by many the "father of history," had come from Greece, and he wrote about a great labyrinth that existed in Egypt over 5000 years ago, near the "City of Crocodiles." He described it in extraordinary terms, saying it had twelve covered courts containing over 3000 rooms filled with hieroglyphs and paintings and was the most beautiful of all buildings, constructions, anything designed in the world that he had ever seen, and he claimed to have seen almost everything from that period of time. There is also a description of a similar area in the Bible. But it was a very special treat to be sitting there, listening to these remarkable women who are my teachers from different indigenous traditions talk about such a labyrinth in such a sacred way.

Today we have nothing from that labyrinth except a few histories that have been written. But archeologists using 'sub-surface surveys' have found what they believe to be massive ruins covered by tons of sand near Hawara in Egypt, along the Nile River. They believe these ruins may be what remains of the labyrinth that Herodotus visited.

There have been quite a few very incredible sightings of spaceships, as they have been described, in and around the area, except that they were landed. They were on the earth, of the earth, and they were beautiful. The people of the Labyrinth, wherever they came from, knew many things or they could not have built such an amazing place. Likewise, the Egyptians could not have built the pyramids as they did without much knowledge and wisdom, yet we are taught to consider everything before the modern era as "primitive."

"Whether that was shared with Atlantis is a question, I think," Agnes said, her eyes beginning to glow as the sun set, and she seemed to fade into her memories for a few minutes, as if remembering the most beautiful vision on earth. She stopped then, moving from the labyrinth to talk about the incredible green delta of Egypt and how the Nile had been a different river then. It had always flooded at a certain time of the year, to take care of the farmers and take care of the growing times. Then came the wars. Then came the bloodletting. Agnes looked at Betty, nodding her head.

Betty said, sarcastically, "Gee, it doesn't take you long to describe this, or anything. I think I am going to get some dinner, and I'll come back and maybe you'll have gotten to Cairo or Memphis."

And I thought, *Wow, I had no idea that Betty knew so much about Egypt. Why would she know so much about Egypt?*

Agnes looked at me and said, "What was the feeling that you had when you were in Egypt? What was the first sense you had when you arrived in that beautiful place?"

And I said, "I had the sense that I was going back to the source, that even though I'd thought I had been at the source in the Himalayas, I hadn't been. I hadn't realized what a journey Egypt was going to be."

I was captivated by what Betty and Agnes were saying about the labyrinth in Egypt. Our knowledge and understanding of the ancient world—and of the worlds that existed on earth in the time before the ancient world—are filled with controversy and misunderstanding, even with the advances in scientific technology and new discovery. Still, there is a feeling that comes over you when you hear the truth spoken no matter how wild its premise. It is a certain sense of knowing and contentment. This is the feeling that came over me as I listened to their fantastic words.

Despite her occasional grumpiness, which is actually an odd sense of humor that purposely takes you off your center so your perspective is briefly altered, Betty Fast Bear has a fabulous appreciation of the unknown and the unknowable that is contagious, and a deep and abiding trust in the knowledge and wisdom that has been handed down to her through hundreds of generations of shamans and mystics. She is a constant source of inspiration and strength and a true blessing to the world.

As we sat there, each of us lost in our own dreams and remembrances, I was taken back to an earlier time with Betty Fast Bear. I had been telling her about an old Celtic tale that a friend of mine, a long, long time ago, had told me. It was the story of a beautiful sacred cow, not unlike the Golden Goose. According to legend, this cow would give and give and give of its abundance. It would give its milk enough for the entire village to have cheese and have milk, butter, and sustenance. Whenever the people went to her, she would give and give, and never run out, and they would save her precious milk, using it with great care and consideration.

The villagers knew this was a sacred cow, a cow that was to be tended to and guarded with great, great care, and they did so for a very long time, each family taking its turn in caring for her through many generations. This cow was a great gift to the village.

One day, the father of the family whose turn it was to look after the cow had to go into town, so he told his son to take good care of her. The boy went and sat with the cow and he was happy because he loved the cow very much. He talked to her and lay down in the grass next to her, and presently, he fell asleep.

As soon as he went to sleep, down the road, from a path through the mountains, came an old woman, and she was a strange old woman. Making sure the boy remained asleep, she came over to the sacred cow that was full of abundance for the village and she began to milk it. But instead of saving the milk, the abundance the cow provided, she milked it through a sieve she had brought with her so that the milk emptied all over the ground. While the boy slept, she milked the cow until there was no milk left, and then she disappeared, along with the sacred cow.

Soon enough, the boy woke up and realized that the cow was gone, its milk spilt all over the ground. Panic stricken, he ran back to his father's house and told him what had happened.

Betty thought that this was a very fun story and she began slapping her thigh and chortling. Suddenly she stopped still, and she pinned me with her fierce eyes, much the way a bear pins you when it happens upon you in the woods. Then she started talking.

"This is a story that talks about the way the 'civilized' world is in its existence today," she said. "People have so much, all of us, your people and mine. We have such wisdom, but we forget how

197

to tap into it, how to move into the place of knowledge. Instead, we hold out a sieve and let the knowledge that is given to us with such abundance seep through it, meaninglessly."

"Yes, but abundance isn't necessarily a bad thing," I countered. "It holds many great teachings for us if we would learn how to see what we are doing. It is not bad to have money or a lovely home. It is not bad to accumulate wealth if you know how to use it in a way that is for the higher good of everyone."

Betty turned her head so that she was looking at me at me almost sideways. I turned my head, also, so that I was looking back at Betty sideways, through narrowed slits. There was much truth in what she was saying. People today go through our abundance like the old woman in the Celtic tale, milking the sacred cow into a sieve until it all finally goes away and is never seen again.

I said to Betty, "To me, the story of the sacred cow is a story about beauty, a story about the beauty of abundance and balance. We all have the ability to create our own abundance. But if we would first create within ourselves a beautiful receptacle to hold that abundance, a clay pot of sacredness, then we would find ourselves living not only safely but also with graciousness and gratitude. There are people who live this way, and they live a much happier life than those around them. You would probably like many of them a great deal."

She jerked her head back like I had just slapped her, and then she started giggling. "You'd be surprised at the people I know and the places I've been, Little Wolf," she said.

Probably not, I thought. *Probably not.*

All of a sudden I heard a great booming sound that seemed to come from directly behind me, and I crashed back to the present, scared nearly out of my wits.

"What was that?" I wailed, shaking my head and blinking my eyes, terrified.

"What was what?" Betty Fast Bear asked innocently.

"That awful percussion I just heard. It sounded like a bomb just went off right here on the porch," I said, looking at Betty, Agnes and Ruby suspiciously. Agnes was looking at me in a very strange way.

"I didn't hear a thing," Ruby said smugly, and Agnes started giggling.

"That came from within you, Little Wolf," Agnes said. "You must have been very far away, to come back with such a thud."

"Oh, she was thinking of the story of the sacred cow," Betty laughed, slapping her thigh.

"Will you stop doing that to me?" I demanded. "My thoughts are mine. Do I climb inside your heads and listen to you thinking?"

"I was right there with you, Lynn," Betty said to me. "We were thinking of the same thing. That's how I knew where you were. We were there together."

Tears started spilling from my eyes, and Agnes said to me, softly, "What is it, Lynn? What's wrong?"

"There is so much beauty in this world," I said, drying my eyes with my sleeve. "And so often, people just won't see it."

"Well, maybe you're not so hopeless after all, Little Wolf," Betty said. "'Civilized' people so easily forget the beauty around them. They don't see it because they are so intent on milking that cow of abundance, yet they have so little to show for it within their own spirit."

"Yes," I said. "Beauty is what feeds our spirit. Have you ever seen the magnificent painting that Winona has created on her walls? Beauty is what gives us the truth of our lives, not a sieve where abundance and milk drain into the ground and are never seen again. What a beautiful spirit she has. What beautiful spirits all of you have."

I talk a lot about the truth that is found in beauty. It is truth for the spirit and truth for the soul, and to me there is no higher truth. If you lose your sense of beauty, then the truth becomes ugly and stale and boring; it lacks luster, and color, and depth. I don't want to listen to things that I do not need to hear because it dulls my hearing. I don't want to fill my life with meaningless chatter. I want to reach out to the world, across all boundaries, and find the sense of motivation to be creative, to explore the mind of another person, to grow into a place of intellectual and interesting discussion.

There is a place within all of us that Meister Eckhart talked about in his writings. I don't remember the exact quote, but he spoke about that place within us that no one has ever touched, that no one has ever wounded, a place that is unscarred and true. To me, bliss is within that place and it is also that place where beauty leads me. Beauty is the guide to that inner sanctuary, which has always existed within us although perhaps we have not yet opened the door to the sanctuary, thinking that truth and wisdom and beauty are certainly outside of us, in some place foreign.

There is a kind of truth in that, because there is truth and wisdom and beauty that lives outside of us and will continue to live even though we don't see it. But there is also a truth to the fact that the real wisdom of your soul can only be found by you, sometimes with a Master or a guide, someone who can help you discover that sanctuary within you and move into it at will. It is there that you will find the delight of the great gift that your life truly is. We live between the act of awakening and the act of surrendering. The soul is always hungry for beauty. It searches beauty out in architecture, in music, in love, in friendships, in nature. Beauty is what feeds the soul, and discovering new beauty is like a homecoming. When we see beauty, when we touch beauty, we feel like we have returned to ourselves. Beauty meets the needs of the soul.

I truly believe that now, right now, is the time to awaken and find beauty because, in a way, there is nowhere else for us to go in our lives. Politics has become the language of economy and mathematics. In many respects, the things that we have always looked toward for our salvation, for our security, are leaving or have already left us: the specialness of our communities, our common bond, knowing that we are all just human beings, trying to get through life by helping one another rather than helping ourselves to what another person has. We've let the glue that has held people together for eons all spill out onto the ground. In the process, we have lost our innocence.

We live in difficult times, times when we are so uncertain, and the process of that keeps us from the carefree qualities of relaxation and awakening where we allow beauty and things of beauty to happen. Perhaps in fact, the problems that we find ourselves in today could be because we do not understand beauty or we cannot even see the beauty of the world that is all around us. We seem to be enveloped in tapestries of smothered language.

I am reminded of Robert Morgan, who speaks and has written about the difference between glamour and beauty. And there is a great difference. Glamour is an idea of what is beautiful, as in Hollywood and in fashion, not that I don't love it, because I do. But that is not beauty, it is glamour, and the two are a whole world apart.

With all of their gruffness and the weathered features of having lived lives of sacrifice and very hard work, the women of the Sisterhood of the Shields are among the most beautiful women I have ever seen. They radiate a light and a bliss, a sacred serenity that is exquisite, and whenever they walk into a room, whether it is an earthen-floored hut made of woven reeds or the most exotic palace in Egypt, everybody is moved to a higher state of being. When you only fill your vision with things that make you wealthy, spend your time looking at things you really do not need to see and listening to things that only dull your hearing, you lose all sense of proportion and balance and graciousness.

Beauty, on the other hand, is always there. She is waiting for you in hidden, secret places until you come to her and see her. But for you to find her, you have to move into those deep, silent places within yourself. I have always thought that you don't need to go to caves in Tibet, you don't need to go to gurus or other enlightened beings to find your bliss. All you have to do is sit in silence in nature, in a beautiful place, and begin to see that the beauty you see all around you is a reflection of the beauty that is living within you. That is when beauty shows herself in all of her glory, when you begin to recognize yourself in that beauty.

This is what I learned from Betty Fast Bear, Agnes Whistling Elk, Ruby Plenty Chiefs and all of my teachers.

Circling Back: "Fencing In Your Consciousness"

Prophecy is a funny thing. If we believe in something strongly enough, it is exactly what we are going to create in our lives, whether it has any foundation or not. Still, prophecy has long been a fascination of humankind. Even our modern theologies contain voices of the prophets.

It is one of the miracles and mysteries of life that the knowledge and wisdom of the Ancients have an incredible way of pointing us in the right direction, across the ages. Our languages have changed so much over the millenniums that we have no way of really knowing if our translations of the prophecies are accurate, yet there is much to be found in what the ancients had to say about where we find ourselves today.

The world as we know it is going through a huge shift, from the physical forces of nature and the melting of the polar ice caps to the very core of our societies all across the globe. This is a shift that has been spoken of by mystics throughout the ages as a time of great struggle, and we can certainly see that in the pressures of our world. I sometimes belabor the point, but it is something that we must not forget. The Great Spirit is commanding that we change to a higher level of consciousness now, and we see that everywhere we look in today's world.

In the Long Count of ancient Mayans, December 21, 2012, marks the end of the Mayan Calendar, what some call "the end of days." What that actually means we will never really know because most of the Mayans' texts were destroyed centuries ago. What is so intriguing to me is that along with the ancestors' ability to foresee the chaos of today's world, the ancient Mayans were also able to predict with remarkable accuracy the line-up of celestial bodies that our science tells us is actually going to occur in December of 2012. Regardless of what earth changes this astronomical line-up may portend (and we don't really know because our scientific awareness of the great forces of the universe is very much in its infancy), if we image 2012 as a time of Armageddon, the literal "end of days," then that is what the collective "we" will find a way to create. I don't believe that an Armageddon is truly on the horizon, although we certainly have the technology to make it happen.

Where are you in your life as you live through these crossing times? Are you living your truth? What is it that you are imaging for your life and for your world?

There is no better time to take stock of your life than right now. If you would have peace and tranquility in your life, you will find it in the garden of your own spirit. This is one of the fundamental teachings of shamanism down through the ages.

Beliefs are an important aspect of human consciousness. They are a stabilizing influence that keeps us from blowing around aimlessly, like tumbleweeds on the prairie. They help us to define our own personal point of view instead of what someone else tells us our point of view should be. If you are always letting someone or something else tell you what you should believe and who you should be in this world, you are denying the miracle of your own existence and it is very destructive to you.

What happens all too often, however, is that we end up carrying our beliefs around like a huge bag of stones, a whole bagful of notions that weighs us down, limits our growth and puts fences around our consciousness. Then we cannot see beyond the fences. We cannot see the beautiful potential that is who we are today.

It is important to have ideas and feelings and beliefs. They create mirrors for you that are great teachers. But wise is the person who takes the time to take a good look at her beliefs on a regular basis. Are your beliefs serving you well, or are you fenced in behind a set of beliefs that no longer works for you, that leaves you no room for growth and change?

In about the 2nd or 3rd century A.D., a Christian priest named Tertullian wrote, "I believe because it is absurd." I love that statement for its simple truth. It reminds me to laugh at myself when I discover that I have allowed my belief structures to become so rigid and overbearing that they cripple my spirit and separate me from the great flow of life. That is the catch in having beliefs; it is easy to become so set in them that we cut ourselves off from the marvelous possibilities that life holds.

Always remember that no matter how fiercely you believe something, it may actually not be true at all, as you will discover one fine day, hopefully before rather than after you have invested your time and energy tilting at windmills, like our good friend Don Quixote. Circumstances change. People change as we grow and deepen through our experiences in life. Has your belief structure grown and changed with you? Now would be a very good time to take a look at this. That way, as you move forward in life it will be with conscious intent and purpose.

Do your beliefs fence in your consciousness, put boundaries around your experience of being alive? Why? Is it really serving you well? We live in a world that has been locked into a cycle of warfare for hundreds of years. Why? Because we believe it to be so. We even tell ourselves that, "This is the way it has always been and it is the way it will always be." That is a complete and total falsehood and one that we should get rid of immediately. We possess the capacity to end life on this earth as it has been known for millenniums, yet people today walk around wearing headphones because they can't stand to know their neighbors. "I am right and you are wrong, and in the name of my god, I kill you."

The decisions that we must make at this particular point in time are so momentous that it is impossible to grasp their full import. At the same time, they are really quite simple. Our modern world also loves to tell itself that, "This is the way God intends it to be," whatever "this" is that we are fixated upon at the moment.

I beg to differ on both counts. We have become so separated from Mother Earth, from one another and from the heartbeat of the ancients that we really don't have a clue about how it really is, let alone how it "always has been." We have become so separated from the Divine that we often don't really know what is in our hearts.

It is a great privilege to be alive at this time in human history, when we are literally birthing a new consciousness into the world. The possibilities that exist for us today are blessings about which many past generations could only dream. What part of that "dream" are we going to carry through this crossroads with us? Is it one that is limited by the confines of what we think we know or believe life to be?

Once you fence something in, you place limits upon it. Whether it is your own consciousness, scientific discovery, or whatever, putting fences around it stops its growth. Are we really certain that the world we see today is what we want to carry through the crossroads and into the future? Or is it time to open ourselves up to the possibility that what we see today is truly not "the way it always has been and the way it always will be?"

Something to think about.

14

ANI

Ani, from Katmandu, Nepal, stood in front of the bus stop near the Inn of the Loretto in Santa Fe. My skin prickled. Suddenly I felt closer to the weather. Every moment of past meetings with Ani rushed through me and then there was stillness, pure and clear, like a flower petal. I pulled my truck into the driveway of the Pueblo-like hotel. It was summertime.

Ani fit right in with the tourists and the New Mexicans, dripping with turquoise and long silver fiesta earrings dangling below the neckline. Her hair was tied back in a beautiful braided bun. She wore a hat from Nepal, a hand-laced blouse, and long skirt with the blue and red designs from her village.

Ani lives at the foot of the Annapurna Himal in Nepal, toward the Tibetan border. She has been a teacher, advisor, and friend of mine for all the years that I have been part of the Sisterhood, and I had not seen her for a very long time. I had been in Nepal and Tibet with her in the 1980's, learning about life and death and the great windhorse aspect of consciousness, the level of consciousness that you traverse as if riding a wild stallion across the Mongolian steppes. It is the last stage of consciousness before you move into enlightenment.

All of these thoughts raced through my mind. I was so excited to see her that I stopped the truck, leapt out the door and ran to her, putting my arms around her and laughing with her. Tears were in her eyes and in mine. I couldn't believe I was standing in Santa Fe, New Mexico with Ani. The last time I had seen her was in Katmandu, when we had decided to say goodbye on a busy, dusty street outside of the Oberoi Hotel. She had come down with me by Trans-Nepalese bus to pick up supplies in Katmandu and was going to return to her work.

Now, she had come to Santa Fe just during the time of the Folk Art Museum celebration. To say that she fit in with all of the artists who had come from different parts of the world is an understatement. She appeared to be an artist from Tibet, Nepal, or Mongolia, like my friend, Jeannie, who sold her beautiful pen-and-ink drawings of horses from the high plains of Mongolia.

I held Ani a moment and then picked up her cloth bag. It was heavy and full of her belongings, and I put it into the back of the truck. Then I helped her into the front seat and gave her a glass of ice water. It was very dry in Santa Fe and I knew she would be extraordinarily thirsty. I had not picked her up from the airport at her request, because she said she wanted to travel by bus into Santa Fe, as she traveled in her own country.

She was as excited as I was, chattering in broken English, swaying up and down in the front seat like a kid. She handed me a package and I handed her a package. Hers was wrapped in newspaper. She knew I loved gifts in newspaper, so that I could keep the newspapers and read the dates on them.

That was the beginning of long and beautiful days and nights of my making her comfortable as a guest in my own home. This was the first time I had been able to treat her and make her as comfortable as I could think of, building a fire, making something for us to eat for dinner, sitting out on the back patio underneath the high pine trees that towered overhead. She loved it. She was so happy and grateful, filled with an impregnable strength that held us in a circle of sharing and wisdom and humor. Later that night, she put on some soft Tibetan shoes that she usually wore only in her own home. Always when she was out and about, she was in heavy boots and always she had equipment tied around her waist for planting or cutting herbs when needed.

One day Ani and I got up early in the morning and went for a walk up Canyon Road and down to the Santa Fe River. It was very beautiful out and we sat together on a park bench, having a sandwich. Ani told me about her family, some of the people of Chepang who were living in Tibet. She had seen her family recently and she said that the treatment of them was so difficult to live with, because the Chinese were so mean to the people of the village. They stole everything they could get their hands on and made life very, very difficult for the villagers.

And then we talked about politics and the 'ruling tribes' of the world, as she called them—communism as opposed to capitalism—and how very difficult and strange it all was.

"A people work so hard simply to survive," she said. "Most especially, the subjugated people of Tibet have no idea how to change their lives in any way.

"And really," she continued, "we don't wish them to change their lives at this point because so quickly they could all be dead if they tried. At least they are alive."

I looked at her, shaking my head, thinking how sad it is that for centuries and centuries, Tibet had been a holy, magnificent place.

"And it still is," Ani said. The women of the Sisterhood have the most remarkable way of reading my thoughts. "The mountains cannot be destroyed. They cannot take the mountains away from us."

And then she looked at me, placed her hand on my knee and said, "Lynn, do you know, we were climbing up to some of the highest peaks not too long ago, and we found a station that had been built on one of the highest peaks."

I asked, "A station?"

And she said, "Yes, a station that was obviously for the landing of planes."

She said that it was told to her by one of the monks of the village that the people there had seen huge rockets being brought in and stored beneath the earth for later use. Nobody knew when, just at "some future time."

"Well, why would they have rockets? And bombs, too?" I asked.

"Yes," she said. "Bombs, stored at one of the highest points in the Himalayas."

And I said, "That is so strange. Why would that be? There is nothing there."

She shook her head, holding her hands out in front of her in a slicing movement. "It's one of the highest places in the world, if not the highest. Rockets can be sent from those places more quickly than anywhere else because they are already at such a great, great height that they have the opportunity to go further than something fired from a lower position."

I was incredulous. "You mean that they have put launching pads for rockets at one of the highest points in the world so that they can be unobstructed in their launching of force?"

"Yes, that's what we saw."

I have asked many different people since that conversation and, of course, there has been no answer. Western people know nothing about this; probably most people in the world don't know about it.

As Ani and I were talking, I was suddenly filled with a terrible sadness. I couldn't imagine how human beings could be so irreverent of life, so completely unrelated to the magnificence of life force and the powers that truly animate us. The Himalayas aren't for launching rockets of terrible destruction. They have been revered by people for eons as among the most holy places on earth. Ani drew a picture in the sand with a stick and I followed her movements, seeing a dish-like shape.

She said, "When we fly, when we go from one dimension to another, we often see these saucer-like figures in the sky. They hover above us sometimes."

I took one of the paper plates that I had and held it up, swiveling it around as I asked, "Like this?"

She said, "Yes, but with a dome, like this," pointing to her drawing with a stick.

I realized that what she was talking about was what we consider to be a flying saucer. I asked her, "You mean flying shields?"

"Yes, yes!" she said, a big smile on her face, happy that we had understood each other. She spoke in broken English and sometimes it is difficult for both of us to understand each other.

"Have you ever seen them land?" I asked, bringing the palm of my hand down onto the ground.

And she said, "No, but sometimes they will fly in groups of three." She held up her fingers, so covered with calluses and rings of silver and turquoise. Just sitting with her took me into a completely different world, a world of a primitive yet sophisticated quality that we have so truly forgotten.

Suddenly I was in another place and time, a long ago encounter I had with Ani and a Nepalese sorceress that had changed me forever. Ani had not wanted this meeting to happen, but I insisted and she acquiesced. I remembered that the meeting had not gone well, and now I was once again sitting on the ground outside a small hut listening to the Chepang language being screamed back and forth between Ani and this woman, behind the blue, red, and yellow-bangled shawl that served as a door. I was shaking, but the people of the village paid no attention.

Ani came, then, out of the hut, grabbed hold of my blouse and literally dragged me, kicking and screaming, up the hill and back to the road so that we could catch the bus.

I kept yelling, "But Ani, Ani. I need help. She will help me."

Ani spat on the ground and looked at me with such disgust that I shut up. I didn't understand why she was so terribly angry. Finally we got on the bus. She was still furious. She would not speak to me. She fell instantly asleep next to me, with her head down on her chest, waggling back and forth as the bus careened over the ruts of the ancient road. Chickens were flapping their wings and goats were braying.

We stopped in the evening to have some refreshment from a general store. We got out of the bus and Ani took me a few yards away. She took her scarf from around her throat, spread it on the ground and heated some water for some buttered tea that she had brought with her in her pack. Then she looked at me, shaking her head.

She was looking at me that same way now as we sat together in Santa Fe. I realized she was having such fun remembering this, patting her thighs and slapping her knees, laughing the way these women of the Sisterhood laugh, which is like no other, deep from their bellies, deep from their hearts. I found myself going back into the dream of our earlier time together, as if she was pulling me.

Ani sat there in such a fury as we drank our tea. And then she said, "You had a great scientist in your world and his name was Einstein."

I was shocked to hear her say that.

"Einstein? You know about Einstein?" I asked.

She shrugged at me. "You know, he had great power. He had great ability to go to the other side and to hear what the spirits were telling him. A great power came into him at that time and I want you to know something. He could never have misused that power to hurt anyone. It would have been impossible. True power only comes in to those who would never misuse it. The sorceress in that village was evil, and she intended to hurt you. So her power was a mirage, because no one who has true power would ever consider harming another. No one. Now do you understand my anger? You got taken in and you were ready to give away your power," she said to me, taking her finger and pointing at my chest, digging it practically into my ribs.

"How dare you have given away that kind of power? I am ashamed," she had said at the time.

Suddenly, sitting back on my heels, I could see the stupidity of what I had done and how silly I had been.

"Remember that. Never, ever, forget that."

"It is true," Ani said. "And all your fear of someone trying to hurt you went away upon that realization. And light came back into your soul, just like the sun, these beautiful rays of light streaming down onto us now," she said, pointing skyward. "You were right that day."

I thought back on it and realized that surely it was true. I gained great courage from that experience after realizing that, first of all, no true healer wants to frighten you. That is not the intent or the way of a true healer. The woman had worked so hard to find places of distress within me that I was convinced they were really there, that I was in need of her 'healing.'

A true healer wants you to feel loved and comfortable and encouraged so that you can relax and let healing happen. Ani had shown me that Einstein could never have had the mental powers he did if he intended to hurt anyone with them. Power would never have come to him. Perhaps others would take that extraordinary knowledge and misuse it, but he could not have.

"I have been so excited by remembering that experience," Ani said later that afternoon as she walked around my small living room and rearranged my flowers like my mother would have done. "Now, I want you to take me into town. I want to see this 'Santa Fe.' Show me something special."

As we went into Santa Fe, I thought, *I know right where I will take her*, and we headed toward a trader I knew who had been in Tibet years ago, when the Chinese had first come in and were destroying four to five thousand monasteries, one after the other. He had been able to save some of the tiger doors that led to sacred sanctuaries within the monasteries. I knew that he had once had many hundreds of the doors and hoped maybe a few would be left since last I was there. We went into the shop and I saw my trader friends. They were all very glad to see us. They thought that Ani was a woman from the folk art show.

I said, "I want to show my friend the tiger doors. Do you have any left?"

And he said, "Oh, yes."

This antique shop carried so many old things from India, Tibet, Nepal, and areas around that part of the world, Asian things, carved wood elephants and horses, hundreds of tables, assorted painted figures, hundreds of Persian rugs rolled and hanging from every rafter. He took us back through a labyrinthine set of hallways lined with paintings and rolled up rugs and old, beautifully painted carousel horses. Presently, we rounded through a heavy, thick doorway, as if we had been transformed from Santa Fe into Katmandu.

Ani was walking slowly and placing her hands against the doorjambs, looking at things. "Ohm, Ash."

She was so excited, so pleased. We came to the tiger doors and all of a sudden I watched her aura change into a bright orange with a beautiful blue around it as we went towards the doors, which she had seen instantly. They were stacked together, leaning up against the wall. Each was at least two to three inches thick, made of heavy, heavy wood. They were not tall doors. They were short, maybe 5 feet tall, different heights, and they were exquisitely painted.

They were ancient. You could see that in the grain of the wood and its polished quality that comes only with age. And there were the paintings on these doors of tigers, magnificent paintings of ferocious tigers, running, moving straight towards you, all different aspects of tigers. Ani looked at them and shifted from an incredible relief to be seeing them into anger. She went up to them and pulled a couple away.

My trader friend said, "Oh let me do this for you," and he placed some of the doors for her. They were heavy and he could barely lift them.

Ani placed her hands on the hinges and, finally, one door arrested her completely. It was a tiger with his tail wrapped in the sign of infinity, moving towards you. Its eyes looked straight into hers. She went to the painting on the door and placed her cheek against it and stood there for quite some time, breathing deeply. I watched as her energy field shifted. It was as if she pulled the energy of the door into herself and experienced the history of the door. It was as if it spoke to her.

She told me later that, in fact, the doors had spoken to her and that they had been so happy to see her. That may sound crazy, but I think it's the truth. Ani is an extraordinary shaman healer, "of high degree," as they say in the Australian Outback. A piece of hewn wood, carved and hand-painted like this with such sacred intent, that had remained for centuries within prayer and droning and music and silence, the holy silence of the ancient monasteries and the power of the Himalayas moving through them for heaven knows how long, how many ancient years of joy, enlightenment, and peace. Why would anyone even think that these doors would not have spirit, that they would not be as sanctified as any holy vessel?

Finally, Ani turned to me and said, "Come, we must go."

She nodded to the men who were bowing deeply to an obviously sacred woman and walked quite quickly out of this shop. I hurried to keep up with her.

Outside the shop, I said, "Ani, what's wrong?"

She stopped and looked at me.

"Those doors have been saved and you should have one of those doors," she said. She continued, "But know well that these doors should not be here. Nevertheless, here they are.

"It is the sun, the sun coming over the Himalayas into your place of power," she said, putting her hand over her solar plexus, "the *chi*, your shaman center, your place of power." She used several additional words, words that I had not heard before. "It is the symbol of the sun, tiger, enlightenment, the windhorse galloping, charging into you with the power of the sun, the last stage of enlightenment before peace comes."

She took a deep breath, placed her hand over my heart and said, "Thank you. *Namasté.*"

Circling Back: "Return of the Goddess"

When we speak of intelligence, most often we are speaking about matters of the analytical mind, our ability to learn, plan and reason, to store, retrieve and apply information through our mental faculties. As with most things "of the mind," this kind of intelligence is considered one of the most valued aspects of our existence.

I have a somewhat different perspective on "intelligence," one that grows out of decades of study and work with the Sisterhood of the Shields. To the shaman, the mind is a tool, a glorious tool, to be certain, but still only one tool among many that humans have at our disposal to guide and inform us in our journey through life.

My understanding of intelligence is based on the knowing of our *body-mind*, the place within us and at the center of our existence where we are one with the Great Spirit and all of life. It is the place of the *chi,* the place of the Tao within, our shaman center, around our navel. This knowing is not clouded by the doubt, criticism, and judgment which are the hallmarks of the mind.

The body-mind is where we go to draw upon our intuition, that certain knowing which comes from our ability to gather information from the unknown as well as the known world in a way that is not mental. It is through your intuition that you can walk into a crowded room and know instantly whether or not this is a safe place for you to be. Whereas the mind tends to confine itself to the known and knowable world, incessantly seeking out proof for every thought that it has, intuition is the sure sense of knowing that comes with being completely present and in the moment, free of the distractions and mind chatter that block our ability to receive the wisdom and energy of the universe and apply it in any given situation.

Intuition is the intelligence of your body-mind, which is located near your navel, what shamans call our shaman center or power center. This is where you feel what is true with the source of your being, without reasoning it away and becoming filled with doubt. Intuition is what keeps you out of trouble even as the mind is busy denying intuition and getting you into trouble.

Truth lives within your heart and your soul. It informs your mind, rather than waiting for the mind to make up its mind about things. It is through intuition that you have access to the great voices of spirit that exist on so many levels of existence, voices which the mind usually dismisses as a matter of course.

Intelligence is a remarkable thing. It is a wonderful and even a unifying concept, even as it means something different to everyone every time we use it. It is a concept that speaks to potential, with all of the hope and excitement that potential brings with it.

Sometimes we limit the word "intelligence," as when we use it to measure a person's capacity for intellectual learning based upon what they already seem to know. Other times we use it to imply the wide open possibilities of all of life, as when we talk about the intelligence behind "intelligent design," the ability of the natural world to adapt and accommodate itself to any eventuality. Lately, we even talk about artificial intelligence, our own ability to design machines that can replicate and perform many of the mental processes often more quickly than we humans can.

To me, intelligence is found not in what we know, don't know or are capable of knowing intellectually. It is found in the creative brilliance with which each of us handles the riddles of life every single day, from the biggest complexities to the smallest perplexities. Some of the most well-educated, sophisticated people I know make some of the biggest miscalculations in living that I could ever imagine, while so often it is the least complicated souls, without layers and layers of conditioned and institutionalized learning, who have the most profound and brilliant insights into human nature and what it takes to make life work.

A college education is a marvelous thing, indispensable, really, in today's world. So often the pathway to a college degree is the only place we can go to acquire the mental discipline and the ability to think in an ordered way that it takes to succeed in life, paying attention to appropriate detail. Intellectual curiosity opens us to new vistas everywhere we turn, and the research and analytical skills we learn in school can help us to satisfy and build on our curiosity in every endeavor we may ever pursue. Without curiosity, we stop creating. When we stop creating, we stop living.

At the same time, however, the most important degree you will ever accomplish in life is the degree you create within your own spirit, where you take responsibility for what you know and do not know, where you take responsibility for what you create and choose not to create in life. When you stand firmly in your own spirit, in your shaman center, the center of your own personal truth, there are none of the crippling excuses or blame that so paralyze our ability to function in the world.

It is in your own spirit that you know the truth of what you have accomplished, as opposed to the value that the external world may place on your accomplishments. How often do we see ideas shunned and shoved aside by the prevailing "authorities," only to have those same ideas resurface to solve some of the most complicated problems we have to face?

It is in your spirit that you develop trust in yourself and your abilities, along with faith in the world around you that even though life may be fraught with difficulty today, the Great Spirit has a higher plan for you. All you have to do is stay true to the person you are in your spirit, the person you are in your body-mind at the center of your own existence, the place where you are one with the Great Spirit and all of life. This is not something in which you can major at college. It is something that you will only find through your search for a spiritual understanding of life. To follow this search, you must become open and attuned to the voice of your intuition and the power of your oneness with the world around you.

Imagine waking up in the morning to a world filled with joy and possibility. The sun may be shining, or not. Your bills may be paid, or not. You aren't sure if the kids actually settled their differences, finished their homework, or put out the trash before going to bed, so you don't know what your morning is going to hold. Perhaps someone close to you is gravely ill, or your company is facing cutbacks. But as you open your eyes from the inner world of dreams to the landscape of your physical life, all that you see are the limitless possibilities and wonders of being alive!

Where on earth do you come from? How did you get like this, and can we bottle you?

Many years ago, I asked my teachers to let me come live and work with them in the majestic beauty of the natural world in which they live, away from the crushing pressures of modern civilization. They told me, "No," that was not my pathway in this lifetime; I had struggled and worked too hard to find a deeper meaning to my life and my world than to run away in search of an illusion.

They said, "Lynn, when you can learn to sit like a sacred Buddha amid the pandemonium of your life, never leaving your center, counting your bad points as well as your good and exploring your weaknesses until you discover the great strengths which they hold, then we can talk about how well you might do amid the pandemonium of ours, if you still wish."

They were right, of course, as they have been about all that we have done together. I am very much a person of this modern world. In fact, I rather like electricity and running water, secure shelter from the extremes of nature, getting on a plane to go to the far corners of their world and then returning to the comfort and familiarity of my own home.

There is so much about this modern world that needs to be fixed, especially our acceptance of the inevitability of war and our utter disregard for the sanctity of cultures and traditions other than our very own. It is sometimes overwhelming. My greatest passion in life, however, has always been finding seeds of enlightenment so that I can sow those seeds as far and as wide as possible. It is my chosen pathway in life.

As a shaman woman, I have learned to look at my world in terms of both the reality of what is—not to be confused with what I wish it could be—and more importantly the energy that is driving it to be the reality it has become. A shaman is one who has learned to choreograph energy toward a higher purpose in life. In order to choreograph energy, you have to first understand what that energy is.

When I look at the energies that are driving the chaos, confusion, and destructiveness of our modern world, I see a world that is utterly out of balance, from top to bottom, so out of balance that it is out of touch with the life force itself. It is a world where there is seldom any balance between the energies of the sacred masculine and the sacred feminine, a world that is often bereft of feminine consciousness altogether. This world is the culmination of forces that were put into play many thousands of years ago when the rise of the patriarchy forced the goddesses of the universe underground.

The loss of the sacred feminine in our lives is a disaster, for this earth on which we live is a female planet. Mother Earth is the great womb for all that lives upon her, human beings included. A seed falls to the ground and she receives it. The sky gods send rain and sun down on her and she receives them, awakening the nutrients within her. She takes them into her womb, where a great mating of the masculine and feminine powers of nature takes place. In this way, the seed is transformed and life on earth is born. How can we humans possibly expect to survive, let alone thrive, without both the vibrant feminine and the vibrant masculine consciousness that facilitate life on earth in the first place?

In the shaman way of understanding things, just as life on this earth relies on a mating of the masculine and feminine forces of nature, all people carry both a male and a female shield, two very different sets of energies that depend on one another for their ultimate fulfillment. The male shield is analytical and outward oriented, forceful and aggressive although not in the patriarchal way of domineering control that we see so often today, which is actually the result of a very wounded male and female shield. The female shield is intuitive and receptive, going within to the place of introspection and dreaming to receive wisdom and then expressing love and understanding back out into the world through intuition and creativity. The male god brings his driving force to the divine feminine's powers of intuitive creativity and receptivity. Both are equal warriors in the fight against ignorance. As the power of the masculine explodes and the power of the feminine implodes, the sacred spiral of life is set into motion.

The women of the Sisterhood all say that the crises and conflicts we now face are actually part of a great shift in energies on this planet. It is a shift marked by the awakening of the Great Dreamer God, which signals the winding down of the cycle of the patriarchy as the goddess returns to our world in harmony and balance with the male gods of existence. It is a shift which will bring the driving force of the masculine shield back into balance with the receptive powers of the female shield, and restore the great feminine powers of intuition and conscious dreaming that have been maligned and devalued for so very long. It will also restore our ability to dream a better world for ourselves instead of relying upon the vagaries of someone else's dream for us.

Beneath today's pragmatic, male-oriented reality is a whole other world of power that can be reached only through imagination. Inspiration so often comes after a period of reflection, during which the seeds of creativity are planted. It is the feminine trait of contemplation that brings you to the altar of your imagination, the place where all things are possible, for what you imagine is, indeed, real. If you can dream it, you can do it. Just ask the Wright brothers; ask any of the great artists, inventors, musicians, the builders of our world. Even the greatest scientific inventions begin with a dream; they begin with someone saying, "You know what, I have this idea that what we've come to think of as impossible is actually quite possible, after all."

So imagine: you wake up in the morning to find a stirring deep within you, a peace and a contentment that animates your entire existence and fills you with joy and possibility. You know that no matter what may happen—for life is always going to have its ups and downs, its struggles as well as its rewards—you and your world are going to be alright. This stirring is the power of the sacred feminine being reborn into this world through you, in balance and harmony with the sacred masculine. All you have to do is open yourself and receive her into your consciousness, become receptive to new ideas and new possibilities. The goddess has returned to your world, bringing the energies of life back into balance, and all of the possibilities of life are once again within your grasp.

15

TWIN DREAMERS
Bitter Spring

TWIN DREAMERS AND I were sitting by a pond of bitter water. It was called by the Indians a Bitter Spring.

We had been sitting there for some time, underneath the cover of nearby poplar trees. Deer had come down. Obviously not caring about our presence, they pawed in the water and then ran away, knowing without a moment's indecision that the water was poisoned. It had a strange look to it. You could see your reflection in it, like a blackened mirror.

The sky above was turquoise with the clouds floating in puffy herds, like my dreams, but the water was black. I could close my eyes and hear the buffalo running a long time ago. I could remember when Bitter Spring was clean and pure. *What had poisoned it?* I wondered. I could see in my memory a Native brave wearing a white, beaded breastplate and a band around his head, holding his long hair out of his face. He was riding a beautiful blond and white pinto mare, her ears listening to every word that he said. He looked at the water and he prayed. His mare was nervous and wanted to get away. Soon he was gone, out of my memory.

I took a deep breath and settled into the earth where I was sitting. For a moment I never wanted to move again. I just wanted to sit there in this strange place, a place that in a sense was forbidden, certainly to the animals and certainly to life.

"*Vitalis,*" I said to Twin Dreamers, who had been staring at me with a vague smile on her lips. "*Vitalis.*"

"And would you please speak English?" she said.

"*Vitalis,* life force. That's what's missing in that pond. And if it could, it would take the life force from anyone who would touch it."

"Ah, a good lesson for you," she said, tapping a stick in the sand. "Why are you so fascinated with this place?" she finally asked, her elder face dark and shining silvery brown in the shafts of sunlight coming through the branches of the trees.

"It seems that I should know the bitter springs in my own life," I said. "But so many times I just jump into the water, not seeing it, not observing carefully enough, and in I go."

"And then you're poisoned," she said.

"Yes."

Even the butterflies would not touch the water. I was looking at a beautiful orange Monarch, with tints of gold and black etching around its wings. It came down near the water and flew quickly away, not even touching it. *She knew, but did I?*

As if reading my mind, Twin Dreamers looked at me and said, "Yeah, she knows, but you don't. Why is that, Little Wolf?"

I took a deep breath. "Maybe I am just really stupid."

Twin Dreamers laughed and I laughed too. In part, it was true. I wasn't stupid, but I could be desperately naïve.

"You're like a horse," Twin Dreamers said.

"What do you mean?" I asked.

"You go along a trail and you see something that you haven't seen before, a piece of mica shining in the light, and you shy off to the side . . . jump, jump, jump. Then you see that there is no problem. There was nothing there that could hurt you and you trot back onto the trail, time and time again. Then, however . . . ."

"I know, I know," I said. "There is something about this spring that makes me feel sad."

"Well," she said, "look at your reflection in the spring. It actually shows a mirror-like finish and you can see yourself quite well. Come on, get up. Go look in that water."

"I don't want to, Twin Dreamers. I don't. For some reason it strikes a chord of fear in me."

Twin Dreamers took my hand. She said, "Come on."

I stood up. My legs were cramped from sitting there for I don't know how long. She pulled me toward Bitter Spring. The sand was dry around the edges, no mud, nothing to get caught in like what had happened to me with Zoila in the Yucatán where I had gotten stuck in quicksand.

I stretched out my leg and tested the water. Then I walked up to the edge of the spring. There was an outcropping of rocks and I sat down on one. Twin Dreamers paced around, her long black-gray braid swinging from side to side, showing her agitation. She never stayed in one place for long and this was definitely not a place she was going to stick around.

"Well," she said with impatience, her stick still in her hand. "Come now, let's learn something before dark."

I finally looked in the pond and saw my face very clearly, my disheveled hair, straight, long, and blond, that had been blowing in the wind.

"My hair used to be curly, Twin Dreamers."

"Yes, I know, Lynn. Things do change with time, you know."

"Yes, thank you for reminding me. I'm looking now in the pond," I said.

"It's a spring. There's a difference," Twin Dreamers said.

I took a deep breath and sighed. "I know. It's a place of emergence, but it's dead. What does that mean?"

"I don't know," Twin Dreamers said. "Why don't you answer it? That's what I'm waiting for. I'm getting hungry. Come on." She poked the stick in my ribs.

I looked in Bitter Spring and almost jumped away. Looking back at me was a very young, beautiful Native girl. She was dressed in white. I could see her as clearly as if she was standing in front of me. She held out her hands.

"Come," she said. "Come join me. I want you to join me in this dark water. Come. We'll swim together and I will teach you many things."

She held out a sacred pipe. I was stunned.

"You are a goddess woman," I said. "You are like a Siren from ancient Greece. You're trying to seduce me."

She stared at me through the water and then began to laugh. The sacred pipe disappeared and her beauty along with it. Suddenly her young face was lined and creviced. Her teeth were the color of the water, broken and ugly.

She laughed at me in a jeering way and said, "You will come. Just give it time." And she disappeared.

I sat back and looked at Twin Dreamers. After several minutes, I said, "What was that?"

"What, you have never seen a ghost before?"

I said, "Yes, but I usually call them spirits."

"Whatever you call them, tell me what you saw."

I told her that the woman I had seen was young and very beautiful, and at first I had wanted to join her. She was quite seductive. Then I realized that somehow this pond was a gateway, like so many things we do in our life, like so many things that taunt us and bring us into their energy field. People who pretend to be so kind and loving and generous, and so often trick you.

Twin Dreamers chuckled to herself and sat back on her haunches. "Well, Bitter Spring. Talk to me about that."

"It is a place of emergence and yet it is dead. Very contrary. So perhaps this is a backward teaching, a *heyoka* moment where you come to the spring thirsty, and there is, literally, 'Water, water everywhere and not a drop to drink,' as Coleridge said in his poem."

"And of course, the thought of water made you even thirstier. Then you look into the poison and you think 'a place of emergence.'"

"I could emerge into death," I said.

"Yes," she said. "Life and death, a very thin line. An arrow of great distinction separates you from death. You pick it up and look at it. You look at the point, poisoned on the tip, not unlike the spring. And yet, when you shoot that arrow and it kills an animal and you eat that animal, it is part of your survival. What about the spring?"

"Well, it takes you by surprise. It is a trickster element. If you are not aware, it will kill you. Your instinctual nature is immediately awakened. I see where I have followed that beautiful maiden that I saw in the pond. I have followed her so many, many times. I'm tired, Twin Dreamers. I don't want to do that anymore. I see this teaching and feel it so deeply inside myself. I'm not sure that I can describe it. I just know that the blessing part within me has been touched. Gently I have caressed that place within my own being, and I have made a pronouncement to the Great Spirit that I will take careful, true steps on the trail, on my path as I follow you and the rest of my women in the Sisterhood. At some point, I need somebody by the bitter spring. I will be truthful, but I will also let people learn from their experience. I won't take it away from them. You did not tell me not to be here, not to go into this pond. I saw it for myself."

"Yes," Twin Dreamers said. "Thank goodness. This is a good thing."

By now she was walking in circles, eyeing the trees for a low-hanging branch. Before I knew it, she was crawling up a tree and onto a branch, sitting on it with her back against another, swinging her feet like a young girl.

"Well, I guess that's it for now," said Twin Dreamers.

"Oh, Twin Dreamers, don't disappear on me. Let's go eat something together. Something good, that is not poisoned."

"Yes," she said, "what a good idea."

She jumped down from the tree. Her antics were always so surprising—surprising like the bitter spring—always putting me on my toes, making me aware, making me learn.

Circling Back: "Risk-Taking and Laziness of the Soul"

"The world is a great book, of which they who never stir from home read only a page."
— St. Augustine of Hippo, A.D. 350-430.

We live during a profound time in history. It is a time when we have at our fingertips all of the possibilities of human existence.

As I look across the landscape, I see a world filled with peoples and cultures that are astoundingly rich in their creativity and diversity. I see art that feeds even the most parched soul, science that inspires the imagination to ever higher levels of possibility. I see a natural world filled with so many wonders they take my breath away. Through the beautiful marriage of human ingenuity and the abundance of Mother Earth, there is very little that we could not accomplish right here and right now, if we set our minds and our hearts to the task.

And yet, with all of this possibility and abundance, perhaps, in part, because of it, we have grown lazy, afraid of taking risks. The kind of risk I'm talking about is not the risk inherent in parachuting out of an airplane or mountain climbing, investing in the stock market or even crossing the street. It is the risk that happens when you find that what you are doing with your life bears little resemblance to what you've always believed your life could be. It is the risk that is created when you realize that you are squandering your great dream on the distractions of today's world, the risk that is created when you discover that you are spiritually, mentally, emotionally, and even physically unfulfilled. You are now at a crossroads, where you must make a choice: change direction or give up on your dreams.

A crossroads is a place of great power if only we could learn to look at it through eyes filled with possibility instead of fear. It is a place of power because it is a place where choices must be made and acted upon, otherwise you remain at the crossroads until you wither up and blow away in the wind. Making a choice generates movement. Movement creates energy, and energy creates power, the power and energy you need to move through the crossroads with vision as your guide.

This is the risk I am talking about, the risk of living on the edge of your awareness where you truly push the envelope of all the possibilities that are before you.

The laziness that we have fallen into isn't necessarily apparent to others, even to ourselves, for we live in a highly-charged world that is filled with enormous pressure just to keep a roof over our heads and get our children to school. I am talking about spiritual laziness, laziness of the soul. You could be a person of great energy and ability and still be lazy in your spirit when it comes to taking responsibility for your life. "Laziness of the soul" comes from standing at a crossroads and doing nothing if it is difficult or challenging, doing nothing, particularly if it feels risky.

This kind of laziness happens when we think that enlightenment may not be real, and so we hedge on making a commitment. We put the experience of enlightenment into a little corner of our lives but mouth prayers asking for spirit to come to us, just in case. When you do this, what you are really doing is creating a situation in which you don't have to take responsibility for what you believe. You don't have to take responsibility for shifting your consciousness, for the change that is inherent in living a sacred life.

It is the same kind of laziness that happens when you don't manifest your acts of power into the world because there are no guarantees of success; or you are afraid it will be too difficult before you've even tried to push the envelope, or something unexpected happens that challenges you in some way, perhaps demands more of you than you had anticipated. You want to do something special with your life. You dream of doing it and you know that it is within your grasp. But the road is not as smooth as you had expected it to be. What do you do next?

Always remember this, when you make a bid for power, power tests you. This is something that my teachers have stressed to me again and again, for more than thirty years! Be ready for these tests of power by centering yourself in the commitments you have made, the commitment to living a sacred life, the commitment to manifesting your brilliance and your own unique point of view into the world through your fabulous acts of power.

Then, when you stand at the crossroads of your own life where you must choose between following your dreams or giving up on yourself, what choice will you make? How will you choose risk in your life? Will you push the boundaries of your own existence?

How do you know what is a good risk to take? Remember this concept of risk: wiping away laziness of spirit. If the choice you make wipes away laziness of spirit, then you know it's a good risk to take.

16

HANNAH OF THE LIGHT

ON A SUNNY LEDGE OVERLOOKING the Southern Alps, I sat in silence, contemplating my meeting with Hannah, an elder woman from Russia who has been a part of the Sisterhood for longer than I have experienced this lifetime. Hannah is from the north of Russia, although she lives in different parts of Europe. She is extraordinary, beautiful, and graceful.

I had seen wolf tracks circling a dilapidated and deserted cabin as I climbed up the mountain. The tracks were fresh. I looked around for a scent or sign but saw nothing other than great slabs of grey granite sheeting in crags and reflecting golden sunlight for hundreds of feet below me. On a slope above me, a great horned sheep and his mate stood silhouetted against the sky. The silence was enormous and addictive. I waited. Then, just as I was wondering if I were in the wrong place, I heard her. The jingling sound was unmistakable. I turned slowly, with utter delight, to see Hannah.

"My dear sister," she said softly, with a big smile.

The mountains surrounding us took on life. There was a soft mist in my eyes as the grey shale filled with diamonds and sunlight. The ledge seemed to move slightly in the ebbing wind as she handed me a small glass disk, a pendant with an edelweiss flower held in the center. I placed it happily around my neck.

"From the mountain spirits," she said. "Come follow me."

We walked along a treacherous trail over an outcropping of granite where tiny organic mirrors of shiny mica reflected the golden glow of the setting sun. I couldn't imagine where she was leading me. With each step she took, she swayed as if with the wind. Her brightly woven belt was tied around her waist, the sash decorated with spangles and small seed pods hanging down to the hem of her skirt. It jingled with a soft music, like chimes in the currents of air now billowing around us. Hannah was a slash of statuesque color, her layers of shirts, vests, scarves, sweaters, and skirts of denim and plaid cotton worn over sheepskin boots, a dramatic vision against the mountain's steep walls now turning black in the dusky light.

As we rounded a bend in the path, I saw up ahead an outcropping of carved stone that was high and curved, like the entrance to an ancient place of worship or a shrine for meditation, or even a small cathedral. Several goddess figures and other carvings were placed around the entrance. It was a cave, a sanctuary set into the mountain, and it shone from the interior with what appeared to be firelight. Hannah laughed with me as I threw up my arms in amazement. She took my hand as we entered and then closed the huge, carved wooden doors with a whooshing gust of air.

The doors were made of dark, burnished wood and conveyed a sense of security. I looked around with surprise because there were flickers of light on a domed ceiling carved out of the mountain. It was breathtakingly stunning. This room felt sacred , and I noticed flickers of light that moved like the globes you often see captured by digital cameras. You see the spirits and you see the light moving around behind someone's head, and then it's over in another place but still as perfectly round globes.

"And if you look into the globes of light," Hannah said, offering me a chair at a table, "you will see perfect diagrams within that are always the same. They are diagrams of the life force with which we are all gifted. They inhabit us and they animate us and also they visit us from other levels of consciousness in different ways."

I sat down at the beautiful wooden table, thinking that it would be made out of stone. I ran my fingers across the wood and it felt like there had been so many hands that had rubbed across this table before me. For a moment, I felt the energy or the frequency of others being there. It was a frequency quite similar to my own.

I looked up at Hannah and she laughed, reading my mind, her beautiful face, oh, my goodness, that beautiful face! She looked at once like a gypsy, like a Sherpa in the Himalayas, like a Native American, like an exquisitely sophisticated Latin American woman. It was an interesting read and I was fascinated by it and by her.

She sat down across the table from me and lit a candle. The candlelight drew some of the globes that were floating around on the ceiling down towards us, almost like they were part of the candlelight, or wanted to be, I didn't know. They came around like spirits of place do when you waken them, interested, curious, wanting to know, "What are you going to do now?"

So I simply folded my hands and watched my beautiful friend and teacher and sister, tall and thin, echoing an ancient, perhaps northern Caucasian background not unlike the Bedouin. As I understand it, the Bedouins are not East Indian; they are Caucasian, from the mountains in ancient, ancient times, coming down from parts of Europe, through Egypt, through Sumaria. How you would actually delineate these bloodlines, I haven't any idea, but that was the echo that I saw in her face, the mountains around her spirit.

"What are you doing in Switzerland?" I asked.

With a rather musical Russian accent, she said, "I live in these mountains when I need more light." She lifted her hands to the globes of light, indicating their presence. "I need to meditate deeply sometimes. I need to be in stillness. I need to be in the heart of the mountain for my particular kind of work." She paused and tilted her head.

"And your kind of work," I said . . . I had never known what kind of work she did except that she was called "Light Woman" or "Woman of the Light." *"Here comes Woman of the Light,"* the Sisterhood would say. I never before knew what that meant, as we are all women of the light.

Hannah put her hands down on the table, encircling the candleholder, and said, "Lean over and look at this candle, this sea of light. Think about it as an energy, as a frequency that has been ignited."

I took several minutes, looking at the light and thinking of the transformation that had taken place, how it had happened. In the beginning, there had been a wick made of braided fibers, probably cotton, that was placed in liquid wax which was then left to harden. Now there was a match that had lit the candlewick, causing it to burn. As the heat of the flame neared the wax, the wax began to melt and was absorbed by the candlewick. It was the alchemy that happened when the fibers of the burning wick and the heat of the flame met the wax that allowed the candle to continue to burn for as long as there was a wick.

I knew where Hannah was going with this because I knew that we are capable of creating enough light to light a room in the same way that we are capable of creating enough light to heal our own bodies through the alchemy of transformation. Before meeting Hannah, I had never seen anyone create light with the power of her intent, although I had heard about it from the other women in the Sisterhood. I had heard about it from the monks of Tibet and other sacred places I have been. It takes tremendous training and work to achieve something like that. You can dedicate whole lifetimes to it.

"There is a transformation which has taken place here," I said, finally. "It is the wick which facilitates that transformation, much like what happens with our own bodies when we use the power of our sacred intent to heal ourselves. We can help people by putting green light, the light of the heart frequency, around them to help them heal themselves. You just talked about the candle as an energy that has been ignited. To continue burning, the candlewick has to grow and become stronger. I think that to become more aware, our frequency has to grow and become stronger, as well. Am I right?"

"Very good. Exactly!" she said. "There is no question that there is transference of chemical energy, and this is all about chemical history. Everybody you meet has the ability to use the power of visualization to put light around other people to ease their stress and confusion.

"Now," she said, continuing, "I have spent a great deal of time with the monks in the Himalayas, here in the Alps and a few other places on earth. And these monks have been dedicated for centuries to bringing light into the world, not only on psychic levels but also on real levels."

Everything started clicking in my mind and I thought, *Oh my God, that's how they got light into the tunnels under the Temple of Hathor in Egypt. That's how they had the light.* Under the main level of the Temple of Hathor, there are many long tunnels with a very reptilian feeling. There are amazing writings and hieroglyphs all over the walls, the ceiling, everywhere, very detailed inscriptions. There was a picture of a reptilian man who was giving energy to the priests as they were being initiated. These tunnels are incredibly long, so long that a torch would have burned out deep within them in a very short period of time. There had to have been another form of light for them to have done what they did, and I realized that the light could have come from the light work which Hannah was describing.

She went on to explain, holding a couple of long candlesticks in her hands and stroking them gently, "When you think of light, there is light-atmosphere-condition chemistry created by your thought, and that becomes visible if that is your intention."

I said, "Well, I know that thoughts are energy so I know what you are saying is true, but I don't know how to do that. Do you?"

"Oh yes," she said. "I create globes of light. I create thought shifts in people."

I looked at her and said, "That must be very dangerous, because you can't create something in someone else without possibly harming him or her in some way."

"Yes, there is no question that changing thought forms is a knowledge and a wisdom that has been imparted to the great Lama monks of Tibet by the Masters, shaman people of great light. It is something that cannot be taught to almost anyone else in the world. But it can be done, and it can be done by a power within the mind similar to the lighting of the candle. Watch on the wall over there and see the shadow of you from the candle. See the candlelight and the shadow on the wall. See how much bigger that shadow is. Do you see how much bigger?"

She took out of her pocket a shiny metal disk and I looked at it and said, "That's a *melong!*"

"Yes," she said, surprised. "How did you know that?"

I replied, "The monks gave me one as a gift when I was in Nepal with Ani."

"Oh!" she said. "Its spiritual and mystical uses are ancient, over 5000 years old. It is a blending of eight different metals, the exact amalgamation of which is a carefully guarded secret that is handed down through family lineages. The monks have known these ways of treating metals for many long centuries. It is a mirror that reflects you when you choose to look in it, but it also is a reflector. Look at what happens when you reflect. Here take it in your hands. Now reflect the light of the candle onto the wall and you will see how more intense and bigger it gets," she added.

I said, "Yes, and I can move it around with glass. There are many things that you can use to create a larger reflection, but a mirror is one of the best. The symbolism of the mirror is so powerful. It is one of clarity, complete perception. It is so important."

I took the *melong* and rubbed it with my fingers, polished it and set it at different angles, having trouble at first getting it right. Then I began to reflect the shadows onto the wall with more clarity.

Hannah said, "Your mind is like the mirror of the light. The thought that you bring to the light is reflected and made larger and more intense by the mirror. You are the mirror of the light in this regard. So, let's say that you wanted to transfer thought."

She took a barrette out of her hair, which flowed down her back so that she looked like a young girl shaking her head.

"I'm so excited to share this with you," she said.

And I said, "I am excited to learn this."

But she said, "This is about hypnotism, you know?"

"Mind control?" I asked.

"No. Hypnotism. Hypnosis in that you can make yourself ill or make yourself well."

At this point she got up, lit a fire and made some tea for us. She took awhile and then said, "Here I want you to have some of this bread to eat and have some tea with me and we'll talk about this."

"I am so excited!" I said.

She responded, "If you understand this, you will prosper and you can teach abundance to others. You will realize that there is really nothing in the world that you cannot do. Because if you think it, it will be. People don't understand that this actually is an aspect of feeling and hypnotism."

I asked, "How do you mean that?"

She answered, "It's an act of hypnotism because you know without a doubt that a person can heal another. But you have to convince the person with whom you are working that there is a truth in what they are doing, and this is sometimes difficult. That person has to have faith in you. You have to show them how powerful you are, and that is another very difficult thing to do if you are not practiced or haven't done this in awhile. So, I would like to show you how to do this. Haven't you ever wondered how all of us in the Sisterhood communicate so well?" Hannah asked me, turning in the shadows at the end of the room in a most ethereal way, as if she were about to disappear. I had to hang on to the vision of her, the thought of her as if to keep her from flying away.

And I said, "Yes, I have wondered. I send thoughts to some people and they read them and they know they are from me. But it's rare."

"You can do that with someone, and I'd like to show you how that can be done. The Lamas and the Great Masters and all our shaman sisters have talked about this from time to time because we are so separated, and what a shame that is for us. But in a way, it's exciting. We have developed certain skills, skills that are ancient. They are nothing new. So I want you to look at the flame on the wall and how you can magnify it. It is about the thought, the mind thought that you bring to an idea. When your intent is grounded in the light, there are things you can do with other people to help them find the light within themselves. This

240

is not an ability you will ever misuse, by the way. You are only being taught this because you won't misuse it," she said. She got up and moved the two candles from the table to a bench behind her, where they cast magical dancing shadows across the ceiling.

"This reminds me a little of when I was in Nepal with Ani," I said. "There was a woman in another village who was reputed to have great powers, and I very much wanted to meet her. Ani wasn't happy about this, but she did take me to see her. The woman started shrieking in Chepang the moment she saw me, then she told me that there was an 'evil sorcerer' who was after me, someone who would do anything to harm me, ruin my reputation, ruin my life, and that she was the only one who could help me, but only if I agreed to do certain awful things.

"As it turns out, she was the one who was the evil sorcerer. She was trying to take advantage of me by triggering my fear. And it almost worked, because I fell completely out of my own self and was consumed by terror."

"That's about right," Hannah said. "The reality of the sorcerer's 'power' is that anybody who would really try to kill you using the power of thought does not actually have the power to do that *unless you give it to them.*"

"That's exactly what Ani said," I responded. "She said that I gave away my power the moment I went into that hut looking for somebody with magical powers that I thought maybe I didn't have, myself. At first, I couldn't understand why she was so infuriated, not only with the sorceress but also with me."

"Someone who is powerful enough to really hurt you is actually incapable of even harboring such a thought. That's what this teaching is all about," Hannah said.

"Yes," I said. "We only get hurt when we give away our power, and that is always a choice that we, ourselves, make. No one else can make that choice for us, but it is so easy to lose sight of that. The mind tells us scary enough stories, then you add onto that someone with ill intent trying to trick you into giving them something they want . . . like your power. It seems I've been thinking about this incident with Ani a lot lately."

"Well, perhaps that's because it is one of the most important lessons of our lives, and it can be an easy one to forget sometimes, as you saw in your own self."

I agreed. "It really is, and I've told it many times. It taught me so much. Modern people are always afraid. They believe they always need protection. But protection from what?"

Hannah responded, "Protection from themselves."

"Yes, isn't that the truth?" I said.

"The difference, Lynn, is that I can make you do what I want you to do, and I can teach you about the light at the same time, because I have no intention or desire to hurt you. If I saw that you were in trouble with what I was doing, I would immediately reverse it. That old Nepalese witch could have harmed you greatly, but only because you would have let her in. You would have allowed your fear to make what she was saying become your reality."

Suddenly I had this incredible urge to take off my boots and socks and get up on the table, which I did, feeling the wonderfully cool wood beneath my feet. As if I were a dancer from Spain, I raised my arms above my head the way a Flamenco dancer would do, castanets in hands, and I twirled and twirled on the table as if I actually knew what I was doing. I heard the guitar being played in my ears. I could hear the melody and the sadness, the ever-present sense of death, the *duende*, which is so present in Flamenco. And I danced it as if I had been dancing all my life.

All of a sudden, Hannah started clapping and I jumped off the table, onto the floor where I started turning somersaults, one after the other. I stopped as I ran into the wall. I sat there and thought, *What in God's name am I doing? What am I doing?* And I realized that it had not been my thought at all.

"This was your idea!" I said as I turned to Hannah.

She was laughing uproariously and I was embarrassed. I had jumped up on her beautiful table, clunked around, leapt off the table and done somersaults. Again I thought, *What in the holy world?*

I stood up, brushed myself off and put my socks back on, not saying anything. Hannah poured a glass of wine for me and one for herself in the most beautifully etched crystal goblets I'd ever seen. I looked at them, caressing the glass and smelling the wine, which was "sniffing perfect."

"Wonderful, deep red wine, like blood," she said. "It is the blood of Mother Earth, the wine, the intoxicant of the mind."

We clinked glasses and drank, staring gently into each other's eyes. I was a little out of breath, not believing I had just done all this.

Setting my glass down, I said, "Okay, what was that all about?"

She said, "Well I sent you a thought form. You picked it up, and, as happens, your mind told your body what to do and you did it without thinking, without an objection. You just did it."

My mouth was hanging open and she reached over and put her fingers under my chin to close my mouth.

She said, "Now, do you believe me?

"Yes, I definitely believe you," I said

"I can get you to do anything, anything at all, but that's not the point. The point is that you understand that there is a chemical change within your mind for everything that you do with your thoughts. You affect others and it goes out into the universe. If you have the kind of focus that the *melong* has with the flame, with the fire, you begin to see that there is something powerful here, something for you to learn and enjoy and be very, very humble with. You can learn this, but it is not for making some-body do what you want on a whim. As you know, that is not correct to do, ever. You may not enter someone else's karma or you will take it on.

"What is important is that that you understand the power of thought, that you see that the life you are living is exactly what you have chosen. You, alone, are responsible for your life. In most lives, even with you, Little Wolf, we are responsible for what we create in this life even though it may have been our destiny all along. You had to pick up that destiny, because you don't remem-ber making that choice. You are kind of remembering it now, but very slowly. You will remember more as we go along.

"Realize this. The chemical power of your thoughts, the shift that is happening because you are having a sip of wine, is your chemical balance shifting. There is a change. In the same way, when you hear music, there is a change in the chemical balance in your mind. Why do you think it is that some religions that want to control you do not allow music? They do not allow music, because they know the power that music has. Those sounds, so many of them sacred, can change your world and you may not even know it. Sleep on this, my dear one. It is a lot. Please come, take your wine," she said.

I picked up my wine, as did she. I followed her down a hall-way. She walked me into a beautiful bedroom carved out of the rock with paintings on the walls and a gilded ceiling, a small, lovely room with an actual bed. She showed me where there was a robe hanging for me and where the towels were. She pulled back the immaculately clean bedspread and puffed up my pillows.

Then she said, "You dream well, and I will see you in the morning. I will awaken you at the proper time."

She kissed me on the forehead and closed the doors behind her. There were little sparkling lights, the globes. I wanted to ask about them, but I didn't have time because she was gone. *The globes, I must ask her about the globes tomorrow*, I thought as I fell into bed, sound asleep, most likely, before my head hit the pillow.

Circling Back: "Dancer of Light: Trusting in the Ways of Power"

Language is a wonderful thing. Words create frequency and light. Still, we are so busy using language that we don't stop to reflect on what our lives would be like without it. At the same time, we are often careless in our use of language, leading to great misunderstandings, not only with those around us but also in our own world view and perception of ourselves.

Linguistics is, for me, a fascinating study. We can learn so much about who we are today if we learn where the words that influence us so profoundly originated and how their use and meanings have evolved and changed throughout all of the social, political, and religious upheavals of human society.

The word "perfect" is a prime example. In its original Latin form, "perfect" meant, "to do something completely." Compare this to the impossible mandate we have placed on ourselves today when we think of "perfection" as somehow synonymous with "*flawless,*" which is what you find when you look in any dictionary or thesaurus. How does "doing something completely" and with your best attention translate into doing it flawlessly? Yet we often feel like such a failure when we put our heart and soul into something and it doesn't turn out as we intended, doesn't live up to someone else's standard of what "perfection" should be.

The word "prosperity" has taken a far less tortured route into the modern lexicon, although in today's world we limit our "prosperity" in exactly the same ways that we limit ourselves by the false mandate of "flawlessness." Then we wonder why we are so unhappy in life.

Prosperity comes to us from the Latin: *prosperus,* "favorable, fortunate"; *prosperare,* "causing to succeed or rendering happy"; or *pro spere,* "according to expectation, as hoped." Toward the middle of the 15th century, it came to be more to be associated with good fortune, flourishing, especially in association with the public good.

In today's world, "prosper" still retains the flavor of becoming strong and flourishing, but in all its senses—prosper, prosperous, prosperity—we have really begun to limit our notion of prosperity to the confines of economic well-being, translation—financial wealth.

Do you really mean to tell me that if you work hard and create for yourself a comfortable level of satisfaction and stability—the true meaning of prosperity—that your entire sense of personal well-being is baseless if you haven't become financially wealthy in the process? The crops are in, the harvest was good, but you didn't double last year's net. Does this mean you didn't have a prosperous year?

What are we doing to ourselves with our ever-growing and changing use of the language we speak? There truly is no greater prosperity in life than a heart that is filled with love, regardless of the vagaries of finances.

Do you feel that you have prospered in life, regardless of whether or not you consider yourself financially wealthy? If you do, I celebrate and honor you. If you don't, why not?

When someone is not prosperous, there is a reason for it. Prosperity is more about taking responsibility for your own success in life, however you define success, than it is about becoming wealthy. Is someone who has inherited great financial wealth and spends his time frolicking truly prosperous?

If you do not feel that you are prospering, perhaps it is time to take a look at the blocks within yourself that are keeping you from your own well-being. We are not victims, even when times are hard and nothing seems to be going right. If you are truly not doing well in life, take a look at yourself and see what it is within you that is holding you back.

So often we stop ourselves in life because we have an overwhelming fear of the unknown. Agnes often says that people today are frightened of the unknown because it is so unfamiliar to us. Our linear way of thinking has demanded answers to everything. If something cannot be answered in a tangible, precise way then it must be untrustworthy.

Yet it is within the great Unknown that all of possibility resides. It is in the unknown that possibilities are not limited by judgment, criticism, doubt, all of the contrivances with which modern societies limit themselves. Once something becomes known, it is fenced in by its known and knowable limits. The greatest discoveries of our times come from people asking, "What if . . . ?" and stepping outside the fences to explore something new. That is when the energy light of what they are seeking comes to guide them.

I like to think of it this way. We are all pilgrims on the pathway to the unknown. Is this not what living is really all about, waking up each morning to a world that is familiar and then getting out of bed to a world that is filled with surprises, many of them fabulous and some of them not so welcome? Yet get out of bed we must, bringing with us all of the knowledge and wisdom we have garnered thus far to guide us as we enter the unknown territory of what lies ahead. What an exciting adventure it is to be alive! The key is to be strong in the foundations of your life so that you can enter the unknown in a way that is balanced and grounded, with one foot in the world of the physical and one foot in the limitless world of spirit.

How do you become balanced and grounded? First of all, make certain that your foundations are rooted in your own personal truth. That is where you will find the strength and courage that you need as you move forward. Someone else's truth is what moves them forward, perhaps to a place you really don't want to go. Find your own truth and follow it. It is as easy to create disaster out of success as it can be difficult to create success out of disaster if you are not coming from the place of your own truth.

When your foundations in life are rooted in personal truth and spiritual balance, you discover that trust has moved into your hut and become your ally. You trust in the ways of power and you trust in the light that is the Great Spirit. Everything that lives is made up of energy, and what is energy if not power? The light of the Great Spirit is the greatest power of all. You, yourself, are made of power, so when I say, "Trust in the ways of power," what I am saying is trust in yourself and know that there is nothing that you and Great Spirit cannot accomplish together when trust is part of your foundation.

Move forward into the unknown with the confidence of trust and give yourself permission to make mistakes. We all make them. Mistakes are often our greatest teachers. They help us see what our truth really is, and they force us to draw upon inner reserves that we might not have known we have but for what the mistake shows us. It is all a matter of perspective. You can choose to live your life with fear or you can choose to live it with trust.

One way to look at what is holding you back from your highest good in life is to take a look at your house. Is the energy in your home flowing beautifully, or is it cluttered and disorganized? If your house is cluttered and disorganized, there is a good possibility that your mind is cluttered and disorganized, as well. With a mind cluttered by distractions, how are you going to focus on prospering?

If you need money, there is a reason it isn't there. That reason resides within you. So take a good look at your own feelings about prosperity and about taking responsibility for your own success. Look at how well you accept abundance into your life. Are you telling yourself lies, you want abundance but you do not really believe in it? You can sit around and wish for abundance all day long, but do you truly recognize the treasures that you have already been given and the very real possibilities that are out there for you? My teachers have always said, if you want power in your life, you have to make a place inside you for power to live. If you don't appreciate the gifts you already have, how are you going to recognize the gifts of possibility that are open to you?

Many times as we go on our journey into the uncharted territory of our lives, we get scared. It takes us out of our comfort zone. We live in a society that has conditioned us to expect the worst instead of the best. As a result, we are often so afraid of change.

Change means letting go of what no longer serves you, letting go of old fears and anger. Change means letting go of the veils of ignorance that keep you from seeing your own truth in life. Sometimes we need help in identifying our veils of ignorance, someone who has walked down the trail before us, and that is a good thing. There are fabulous teachers everywhere we look, when our eyes are open and we are willing to see. We are so conditioned by society, and there are many aspects of that conditioning that destroy our life force. It helps to have someone whose vision you trust to help you look through the veils of ignorance that are keeping you blocked from abundance.

Life force is abundant everywhere. If you would, close your eyes for a moment and visualize life force as golden light energy out in the universe, and it comes to your home, to where you live. How does it enter? From which direction? Does it move through your house comfortably?

Take a look at your office, the place where you work to bring abundance into your life. Where is your heart in your workspace? Where is the most important place, your place of wisdom and life force? Is it so cluttered that you can't see your own heart beating there, wanting to be loved? Or is it very obvious where the source of power is and how you are connected to that source of power as you draw inspiration from it throughout the day?

Your bedroom, where you rest at night, is another good place to look. How do you feel in this room? Does the energy flow? These are the things that you need to look at. Stuck energy in your bedroom is good for a lot of sleepless nights, which lead to unfulfilled days.

Are you comfortable in your home? If you are not, change what makes you uncomfortable. We live in a society that seems to pride itself on the ability to complain endlessly and blame others for our misfortune. Don't fall prey to this behavior, it will block you from prosperity, absolutely. Instead, change what needs to be changed to the best of your ability.

If you are allowing prosperity in the form of life force to enter your world, to flow through you and back out into the universe to be replenished, abundance will be attracted to you and come to you. If you have blocks to that energy, you will have problems, so deal with them. Shamanism is about choreographing the energies of the universe. Become the dancer of light and reconfigure your life as an art form, as a performance of beauty. Then ask yourself how you feel about prospering in life!

Conclusion
"Standing at the Crossroads of Power"

WE LIVE AT A TIME of great opportunity in the human experience. There are blessings and possibilities open to us today of which our ancestors could only dream.

At the same time, our societies have grown so complex and riddled with conflict that we are also living under more chaos now than at any previous time in our history.

As I see it, the great possibilities of human ingenuity, creativity, and the development of the truly astonishing technology in which we are engaged today, along with the abundance of our beautiful Mother Earth, have put all of possibility at our fingertips, including the possibility of creating technological and social catastrophes from which human beings, like much of life as we know it, might never recover.

Along with great accomplishment comes equally great responsibility, and it is the enormity of the responsibilities before us that is causing much of the confusion under which we are living. There is also tremendous uncertainty in our world. While nothing in life is ever guaranteed, the kinds of uncertainty we have created today are antithetical to a consciousness of well-being.

We are literally standing at a crossroads in human existence unlike anything we humans have ever faced before. The decisions we make and the directions we choose at this crossroads will affect the direction of life on earth, perhaps, forever, because of the technologies we possess.

A crossroads is a place of enormous power. It is a place of power precisely because it is a place where choices must be made and acted upon. Thoughts are energy forms, and what we think creates energy. As we stand at a crossroads and evaluate our options, preparing to make our decisions, we begin generating energy. As we make and act to implement those decisions, we generate more energy. Energy is power, just as power is made up of energy. So when you stand at a crossroads, any of the many crossroads you face in life, you have within your reach a tremendous amount of power and energy to carry you forward as you choose the path you are going to take, so long as you make a decision and move to act on it. Otherwise, you simply stop growing and moving in life. You become stagnant.

Think about this whenever you feel stuck. Are you at a crossroads in your life where changes need to be made? The need for change is what brings you to a crossroads in the first place. Once you are there, it is time to make and act upon some very important decisions for your life. While it is imperative to take the time to look at your options carefully and make your decisions wisely, the longer you put off facing and making important decisions, the more your energy is going to be drained. So use the energy that exists when you arrive at the crossroads to move yourself forward onto the pathway that best works for you.

The dynamics of energy are truly amazing, for energy creates energy in the never-ending spiral of life in this universe. The simple act of making decisions generates energy. Then you use that energy to begin acting on your decisions. As you do that, you create more energy. The more you get done, the more energy you create. That is why businesspeople like to say, "If you want to get something done, give it to a busy person."

There is a catch, however, in the way you generate and use energy. If you are coming into the crossroads as a victim, as one who judges and blames others, expects everyone else to make and carry out your decisions for you, you are bringing into the crossroads only negative energy. Negative energy has the ability to be a tremendous force in the universe; there is no doubt about that. It is the darkness that defines the light.

The possibilities that exist through negative energy, however, are very limited, no matter how destructive they may be. They are limited by the sheer weight of negativity, which feeds only on other negativity. That is why my teachers say that sorcerers never kill you. They make you kill yourself. They are limited in what they can actually do, so they trick you into doing it, yourself.

Using negative energy isn't going to get you out of a difficult place at all; it's only going to get you more deeply into it. Using the energy of negative thinking, which can make you feel very powerful and important for a moment, isn't going to get you anywhere near the center of the crossroads, which is where the power and energy of all of creation exist. In fact, negativity is only going to drain you of whatever positive energy you have left, for negative energy is completely devoid of the power of creativity.

Creativity is one of the most powerful forces of all. Creativity is the child of love. Love is the life force of the Great Spirit, and it is the most powerful force in all of existence. Creative energy comes when you tap into the life force which is of God.

It is a great privilege to be born at this particular time in human history. The decisions that you make when you stand at the crossroads of your own life and the energies that you use to create and reflect out into the world as you move forward on your chosen pathway are going to have a huge impact on the entire world around you. That is because our very world, itself, is standing at a crossroads. It is a crossroads we all must face. We absolutely cannot allow anyone else to make these next major decisions for our world, any more than we will let anyone make our important personal decisions for us.

We are not victims. In fact, the psychology of victimhood is part of the old paradigm of negativity that has brought us to this crossroads amid so much havoc and destruction. We can choose to stay rooted in this victimization, and the results will not be pretty.

Or we can choose, individually, one by one, until we number every person on earth, to say, "I am responsible. I am responsible for holding up my own dream for a better life, and I am responsible for holding up my dream of a better world." It is when you take responsibility for your life that you really begin to move through the crossroads in very dynamic and exciting ways.

This is the vision that I and my teachers have for our world, that we will move through this crossroads leaving the negativity and victimization of the old way behind us as we reach for all of the light, all of the creativity, all of beauty and joy and power that is the love of the Great Spirit. Reach for the very life force, itself, to guide you into a future of harmony and oneness with all of life. To me, there is no other way.

Sky and Earth

ages ago, the sky
taught us how to live

each song a mountain
an old woman said

each breath a forest

some trees live a long time
because they are not waiting

who will be a dreamer
in the world without fear?

—Jack Crimmins

For the last thirty years, I have been describing my learning and my path. It has been a joy to do this. In continuing my journey, I would be grateful if you would share your insights with me.

Please write me at:

Lynn Andrews
29341/2 Beverly Glen Circle
Box 378
Los Angeles, CA 90077

Please send me your name and address so I can share any new information with you. For more information, please visit my website:

www.lynnandrews.com

I also invite you to follow me on Facebook and Twitter.

In Spirit,
Lynn Andrews

Related Titles

If you enjoyed *Coming Full Circle,* you may also
enjoy other Rainbow Ridge titles.

The Cosmic Internet: Explanations from the Other Side
by Frank DeMarco

Conversations with Jesus: An Intimate Journey
by Alexis Eldridge

Dialogue with the Devil: Enlightenment for the Unwilling
by Yves Patak

The Divine Mother Speaks: The Healing of the Human Heart
by Rashmi Khilnani

Difficult People: A Gateway to Enlightenment
by Lisette Larkins

When Do I See God: Finding the Path to Heaven
by Jeff Ianniello

Dance of the Electric Hummingbird
by Patricia Walker

Thank Your Wicked Parents
by Richard Bach (June)

The Buddha Speaks: To the Buddha Nature Within
by Rashmi Khilnani (June)

Conversations with Jesus, Book 2: An Invitation to Dance
by Alexis Eldridge (June)

Messiah's Handbook
by Richard Bach (July)

*Consciousness: Bridging the Gap Between Conventional Science
and the New Super Science of Quantum Mechanics*
by Eva Herr (Sep)

Blue Sky, White Clouds
by Eliezer Sobel (Sep)

Jesusgate: A History of Concealment Unraveled
by Ernie Bringas (Sep)

*Hemingway on Hemingway: Afterlife Conversations
on His Life, His Work and His Myth*
by Frank DeMarco

Rainbow Ridge Books publishes spiritual and metaphysical titles, and is distributed by Square One Publishers in Garden City Park, New York.

To contact authors and editors, peruse our titles, and see submission guidelines, please visit our website at:

www.rainbowridgebooks.com

For orders and catalogs, please call toll-free:
(877) 900-BOOK